ENGLAND WORLD CUP GUIDE '98

This book has been endorsed by Green Flag Ltd, the official sponsors of the Football Association and the England national squad. However, it is not in any way authorized, licensed or endorsed by any official sponsor of the 1998 World Cup, FIFA or ISL.

First published in 1998 by
CollinsWillow
an imprint of HarperCollins*Publishers*
London

Copyright © Green Flag Ltd 1998

All pictures courtesy of Actionimages except those on the following pages:
Allsport 39 (bottom), 62, 69, 70, 71, 73, 74 (top) 75, 76,77, 80 (right), 81, 88;
Empics 100 (bottom left), 114 (bottom left).

The publishers would like to thank the following for their help in producing this book: Jonathan Pearson,
sponsorship manager of Green Flag Ltd: Tony Henshaw and George Impey of Actionimages; Colin Panter of
Empics for providing additional picture research; Peter Pace and Chris Dighton of Hayters; Nick Wells, Sonya
Newland, Morse Modaberi and Josephine Cutts of The Foundry; and Charlie Richards.

A CIP catalogue record for this book is available from the British Library.

ISBN 0 00 218836 8

Created and produced by Flame Tree Publishing,
a part of The Foundry Creative Media Company Ltd,
The Long House, Antrobus Road,
Chiswick, London W4 5HY.

Printed and bound in Italy by Rotolito Lombarda, Milan.

GREEN FLAG — THE OFFICIAL ENGLAND TEAM SPONSOR

ENGLAND WORLD CUP GUIDE '98

Text by Chris Dighton

Photography by Actionimages

Collins
Willow

Contents

England Back on the Glory Trail

The Greatest Show on Earth

Team Preview

Introduction

Welcome to the greatest show on earth – the World Cup. Bigger, better and more spectacular than ever, there are no problems selling this tournament simply because it lives up to its hype and then delivers more.

For the last two years, 172 nations have been dreaming of Paris and a Sunday afternoon in July 1998; because it is then that football will celebrate the triumph of the new World Champions. It may be Brazil, successfully defending their trophy won in America four years ago, or hosts France coming good. Perhaps it will be one of the other soccer dynasties such as Germany, Italy or England repeating history, or maybe a winner from a brave new country. By this stage, 63 matches will have been played across France, providing a stage for the world's greatest players and a reason like no other to do the business. The World Cup is about the best players and the best teams chasing the ultimate prize – it is the testing ground that turns good players into great ones, mortals into legends.

In a world increasingly divided by dispute, football has become a common language to unite nations; a glorious celebration where even the most patriotic can rejoice at the brilliance of real talent. Media coverage more intensive than ever will mean that no goal is missed, no kick is overlooked, not even a blade of grass will grow without coming under the scrutiny of a camera.

France '98 is the biggest World Cup finals yet, with 32 teams participating – and how the tournament has grown since it was first run in Uruguay in 1930. Then 13 teams were involved, on an invitation-only basis – the fact is that the European nations gave it a wide berth, put off by the three-week sailing time to the host country.

Since then, the four-year cycle of the World Cup tournament has seen the base grow rapidly and the worldwide audience become huge. Yet even so, the winners form an exclusive club of just six countries from 15 finals: Brazil, Italy, West Germany, Uruguay, Argentina and England. Losers who have graced the Final but not won are Czechoslovakia, Hungary and Holland (twice each) and Sweden. This time every side, regardless of the odds stacked against them, will head for France full of hope, if not all that much expectation in the majority of cases. England, however, will hope *and* expect.

Glenn Hoddle and his merry band of 22 players have come through a tough qualifying group – in the process beating Italy to the automatic spot – and will arrive in France on the back of a steadily improving record. Two years ago, England reached the semi-finals of the European Championship only to lose on penalties – as they had done in the semi-finals of the World Cup six years before in Italy. Today the Premiership is perhaps the toughest league in world football, boasting some of the finest imports in the global game as well as a blooming generation of home-grown players. As a result, the standard is constantly being raised and the competition better than ever.

The challenge for England in the World Cup will come from strikers like Ronaldo, Asprilla, Bergkamp and Valderrama, from Del Piero and Raul; from the best of soccer throughout the world. Whatever the outcome though, we are in for a feast of football; one month of the greatest soccer skills, drama and surprise. Let the *England World Cup Guide '98* lead you to France, inform you about who to watch and where to be. Enjoy the show, because you will not want to miss a second....

GREEN FLAG

Andy Cornish,
Managing Director, Green Flag Ltd,
Official Sponsors of Team England

Glenn Hoddle

The town probably ain't big enough for both of them, but then that has always added spice to local rivalry – look at Manchester divided between City and United; look at North London split between Arsenal and Tottenham.

Yet Arsenal and Tottenham have a link that could have considerable bearing on England's World Cup hopes. At Highbury, the Gunners are coached by the Frenchman Arsene Wenger, while at White Hart Lane the memory of Glenn Hoddle stirs fond memories of success and, had it not been for Wenger, Hoddle might never have become a football coach.

When Hoddle left English football in 1987 to play for Monaco in France, Wenger was the club's coach. He recognized that Hoddle was far more than just a supremely gifted player, he was a man with a genuine talent for all aspects of the game.

'When he came to Monaco I don't think he had even considered coaching. I like to think I gave him the confidence to try,' says Wenger. 'I knew he had the right approach and the right mentality. His analysis of the game was excellent and he was always looking for solutions to problems.'

Promotion for Swindon, the club where Hoddle first became a player-manager, was followed by an FA Cup Final appearance for his next club, Chelsea. He signed Ruud Gullit and repositioned the slumbering giants of Stamford Bridge. Next came England and the only job that Hoddle says he would have taken.

Qualification for France '98 is just a continuation of his success: England under Hoddle have direction and style; they look compact and the team is made up of terrific youngsters who are getting better and better. The world, it seems, is Hoddle's oyster. It might be tempting fate – but England has never had it so good.

'I would not be in management if Arsene hadn't pulled me aside in training and told me I'd make a manager,' recalls Hoddle. 'After that I really thought about it. Until then I had no interest in staying in the game after playing.'

Glenn Hoddle was born in Hayes, Middlesex in 1957 and then signed for Tottenham, making his debut against Norwich at White Hart Lane in 1975. By 1978 he was a star of the team, capable of splitting open the tightest of defences with precise and inspired passes. He was a player with vision and the means to realize that vision – plus a wicked and powerful shot. Bluntly speaking, Hoddle was the master craftsman in a world of artisans.

Playing for England came next as Hoddle made a goalscoring debut against Bulgaria in 1979. Spurs won the FA Cup in 1981 and successfully defended it the following year, before going on to win the 1984 UEFA Cup. Then came the 1986 World Cup in Mexico, where Hoddle was an ever-present in the side that reached the quarter-finals before losing 2-1 to Argentina and the infamous Maradona 'Hand of God' goal.

Hoddle was to remain in the international side until 1988, when a 3-1 defeat by the USSR in the European Championship ended his England days. He had won 53 caps and scored eight goals for his country. At Monaco he continued to impress despite some problems with injuries. Opponent Henri Zambelli neatly observed: 'It is difficult to play against someone who seems to have hands in place of his feet.'

Wenger's inspiration, home and Swindon then put his footballing career on a new route. Hoddle, very much his own man, has shirked no challenge and instilled belief in his club teams. He was appointed England coach on a four-year contract in May 1996.

The rise to the top may have been rapid, but that has not mattered. Hoddle has so far been sure of what he wants and been able to get it. Self-belief and inspiring that self-belief in others is more than half the battle....

Tony Adams

Club: Arsenal
Previous clubs: none
Height: 6'3"
Born: 10 October 1966
International debut: v Spain 4-2 (Madrid) 18 February 1987

'You can go over the top with enthusiasm and end up running around like a headless chicken, we noticed that in Euro '96 – we've always had the strength, the determination, the 100 per cent stuff. My philosophy now more concerns using our brains.'

Tony Adams has probably had to face up to more personal crises – both on and off the field, but especially off it – than any other player in the England Squad. It says a lot about the man that he has been able to come through it all, accept his mistakes and change his ways. Today Adams is a happier man, more contented and able to cope.

It also says a lot about him that he is a one-club player, first appearing in the Arsenal team back in the 1983–84 season and becoming the rock around which the club has built its defence. Adams was the kingpin in the 1990–91 season when they conceded a staggeringly low 18 goals in 38 matches and won the championship. Yet there is more to Adams than leading a backline that is rigidly disciplined and technically skilled. He is a defender who can score goals and he is always a threat in dead-ball situations.

It is astonishing to discover that he is just 31 years old, that – injury allowing – he has a good number of years still left in his legs and that his appetite for the game is as keen as ever. It seems that Adams has been around forever. He says that his ties with Arsenal are absolute, that he has no wish to play for any other team.

In part, the reason for Adams being targeted by rival fans is down to how well he does his job. So well that he led the club to an FA Cup triumph over Sheffield Wednesday in 1993 then, the following season, collected the Cup Winners' Cup as Arsenal beat Parma 1-0 in Copenhagen. Adams gave an outstanding performance that night to keep the Italian club's illustrious forward-line of Zola, Asprilla and Brolin in check.

Supporters who see their team thwarted by him time and time again vent their anger in his direction. Learning to cope with that has made him a better person, and in the process Adams is discovering another side of life – he has taken up the piano, he is studying English literature and these days he will leave training not to go and play golf, but to go to the opera or visit an art gallery.

He says that he is getting a genuine thrill from these new discoveries, that because he is able to assess himself he is now fitter than ever, more focused on his job and open to new ideas. As club captain and a man to teach by example, he knows that the lead he is setting is better than ever.

Adams' worth to England is huge. He can marshal his colleagues so thoroughly that any team facing an England defended by Tony Adams and his troops is going to worry.

David Batty

Club: Newcastle United
Previous clubs: Blackburn Rovers, Leeds United
Height: 5'8"
Born: 2 December 1968
International debut: v USSR (sub) 3-1 (Wembley) 21 May 1991

'You are always known for whatever your strength is — mine is getting round the pitch and tackling. People think of me as a ball-winner but I think my passing has been overlooked, I like to play passing football.'

Three clubs in ten years and David Batty can reflect on championships won at two of them — not a bad achievement considering he has not played for either Manchester United or Liverpool.

Batty is a Yorkshire-born pocket-battleship; a tailor-made hero for his hometown club of Leeds United. For years the Elland Road side had been searching for a man to fill the void left by the legendary Billy Bremner and Batty fitted the bill: all aggression, all purpose, driven to win. Leeds fans loved him and a championship was won in 1991-92 when he slotted into a midfield that contained ball-playing artists such as Gary McAllister and Gordon Strachan, with Batty the bulldog in the middle.

The balance was right, but the following season the defence of the title floundered on a dismal away record. Batty, however, was still the key man at Leeds so it came as a major surprise when in 1993, Kenny Dalglish bought him for Blackburn for £2.5 million. It took him only one season to become the club's Player of the Year.

The following year an ankle injury kept him out of action, and his five appearances were not enough to earn him a championship medal; but it was not long before Batty, restored to health after whispers that the mystery ankle injury was going to end his career, was back enjoying his football.

At Leeds he had been the man to stay back to allow the likes of McAllister, Strachan and Gary Speed to go forward; at Blackburn he was being asked to probe forward and was enjoying every moment. Yet when Dalglish left and Ray Harford took charge, Batty's days were numbered.

There was the spat with team-mate Graeme Le Saux, when the two traded punches in a European Champions' League match in Moscow, an incident that Batty says flared up in the heat of the moment and one that had no history or continuing grudge. Whatever the story, though, it seemed that Batty no longer conformed to the Blackburn philosophy and the time had come to move on.

Even so Newcastle, then managed by Kevin Keegan, had to work hard to get him. An original offer of £3.5 million was rejected and then upped to £3.75 million before it was accepted in March 1996. It was a signing that failed to raise much excitement among the locals, but Batty quickly won them over.

So far the talisman magic of the man has not worked at Newcastle where they are still waiting to win their first title since the 1926–27 season, but the club have been close and, given Batty's special touch, might yet make it. An element of his magic would not go amiss with England in France.

David Beckham

Club: Manchester United
Previous clubs: none
Height: 6'0"
Born: 2 May 1975
International debut: v Moldova 3-0
(Chisinau) 1 September 1996

'I know I'm expected to pull myself to a new higher level every time I play; I accept that because that's what I want to do, to perform at the highest level.'

The golden boy of British football, David Beckham exploded on to the scene at club level with Manchester United, stunning football fans with his ability to score amazing goals week-in, week-out.

Many thought he had set a standard he could not maintain, but Beckham has gone from strength to strength. He earned his call-up to the England team for the first of the World Cup qualifying matches – against Moldova in 1996.

Blessed with the ability to score from just about anywhere – his most spectacular goal was scored from inside his own half against Wimbledon in August 1996 – Beckham is a player who is comfortable on the ball and can hit inch-perfect crosses.

Beckham made his way to United from Essex where his parents and two sisters still live. When he was 11 he won a football skills competition organized by Bobby Charlton, who gave him a piece of advice that he has rigidly followed with considerable success – 'shoot at all times if you've got the chance'. He

played for Essex boys, trained with Tottenham Hotspur and had trials at West Ham, but the lure of United was too great, and after finishing school he went north to join the club's training scheme, staying in digs and seeing his family at weekends. It was a golden era as Beckham took his place beside other youngsters destined to become a part of the new United: Ryan Giggs, Nicky Butt and Gary Neville.

United have turned rearing home-grown talent into a fine art form; Alex Ferguson recognizes the value of producing his own players, not just for the expense it saves in the transfer market, but also because of the spirit it fosters. As part of his apprenticeship Beckham had a loan-spell with Preston North End. Beckham's love of the Old Trafford club is such that, even when training with Tottenham, he insisted on wearing a United shirt. He knew moving north would be a major sacrifice – but it was one he was willing to make. In a way it fuelled his desire to succeed.

His first significant contribution for United came when, at the age of 20, he scored the winner against Chelsea in the 1996 FA Cup semi-final. It was a big goal on a big stage, followed by his astonishing halfway line goal against Wimbledon (see left), but Beckham has not been overawed by the success, or the endless headlines that have seen him feature as heavily on the front pages as the sports pages because of his pop star fiancée, Spice Girl Victoria Adams – the Posh one.

Beckham has become one of the leading faces in the new era of football – the age of the satellite star. He is a young man with the world at his feet, and gives every indication that he is ready to make the most of his talents.

Nicky Butt

Club: Manchester United
Previous clubs: none
Height: 6'0"
Born: 25 June 1973
International debut: v Mexico (sub) 2-0
(Wembley) 29 March 1997

'I have more confidence to get the ball and do something with it instead of doing the simple things all the time. I believe my confidence is showing through.'

I t was a big gap that Nicky Butt had to fill – the Manchester United side was without Eric Cantona, Paul Ince and the injured Roy Keane. Most managers would have gone searching, cheque-book in hand, for a proven star.

Not Alex Ferguson. He believes in his young-sters and such belief has been repaid tenfold by Butt, who has grabbed his chance with such aplomb that he

has rocketed from the already considerable height of holding down a place with United, to the international stage. And again he has not been found wanting. His first two games for England were as a substitute and Butt immediately showed that he was not out of his depth, playing in his typically no-nonsense style. If Butt had any doubts about his ability they certainly didn't show.

Brought up through the United nursery, Butt made his debut as a substitute in a 3-2 win over Oldham, and has gradually become a regular in the side. Inspired by Roy Keane, his club colleague, the greatest compliment that can be paid to Butt is that United hardly missed Keane during their 1997–98 campaign.

Butt is a fearless player with a hardened edge and tidy skills and has always proved himself in tough situations, making a strong impact in his first full game for the club – against Gothenburg in the European Champions' Cup back in 1994.

In April 1995 Manchester United were trailing 1-0 in an FA Cup semi-final against Crystal Palace when Butt was thrown into the fray. He was a sensa-tion. United fought back for a 2-2 draw and Ferguson was so impressed that he pledged there and then that Butt would start in the replay.

Capped at Youth, Schools and Under-21 levels by England, Butt has the ability and bravery to score crucial goals, is a willing worker and a player able to read the game well. On the downside, he can be a bit explosive both on and off the field and has been involved in a few scrapes.

If Butt has grown up quickly in the world of professional football, then he is being made to do the same off the field. He knows that both Ferguson and Glenn Hoddle will not tolerate anything less.

A golden future beckons him; he is in the position to shape his own destiny and England could do with his skills, his courage, his heart – and his aggression directed in a positive way.

Sol Campbell

Club: Tottenham Hotspur
Previous Clubs: none
Height: 6'2"
Born: 18 September 1974
International debut: v Hungary (sub) 3-0 (Wembley) 18 May 1996

'I want to bed down in one position, either centre-half or just in front of the back four – that gives you a bite of the cherry at both ends of the pitch.'

The sign of a true international is the ease with which they take to playing for their country – and on that basis Tottenham's Sol Campbell is in for a long and fruitful career. Capped by England as a 21-year-old, he has taken to international duty like a seasoned pro. He has learned the art of keeping some of the world's top strikers in check and has become a key man in England's defensive plans after a startlingly good performance in the 2-0 away win over Georgia in qualifying for France '98.

Campbell has come through the ranks at Tottenham where he has established himself well in the first team. He is the Mr Versatility of White Hart Lane – willing and able to play in defence, midfield and even as a makeshift striker. He is not afraid to make full-impact tackles in his own penalty box and he always pulls it off because of his measured timing and controlled body positioning. His strengths are his

size – in height and bulk – and his astonishing speed. This, together with his superb reading of the game, makes him a pretty complete player.

Born in Stratford, East London, it was West Ham who first took an interest in Campbell. After three months with the Upton Park club, however, Campbell, then 14, decided to leave. Spurs picked him up and, although reluctant to settle down, he took the plunge.

A rare success from the FA School of Excellence at Lilleshall, Sol – christened Sulzeer – has played for England at Youth, Under-21 and B levels, and it was football that made him change his name. While abroad with the England Youth team for the UEFA Championship of 1993, he found the way foreign commentators pronounced Sulzeer too effeminate. His passion for soul music was the inspiration, Sulzeer became Sol, and, with his team-mates around, more often than not 'Sol Man'.

Campbell is still on the learning curve, getting better and better with every match. He recognizes as much and so do Tottenham, who have improved his contract. The boot manufacturers have also signed him up to endorse their products. For a man who nearly gave it all up to become an electrician, it has just gone from good to better – hopefully the best is yet to come.

Andy Cole

Club: Manchester United
Previous clubs: Newcastle United, Bristol City, Arsenal
Height: 5'11"
Born: 15 October 1971
International debut: v Uruguay (sub) 0-0
(Wembley) 29 March 1995

'I don't need to read I've had a bad game. The first person to know that I've played badly is me, but I have confidence in myself to get it right.'

Andy Cole is the one that got away from Arsenal – where he started out as a trainee. He made one appearance for the club before being sent on loan to Fulham, where he scored three times in 13 matches and then eight from 12 games while on loan at Bristol City.

Bristol knew they had found a gem and paid out £500,000 to sign him. It was a move that would have some impact on their fortunes – 12 goals in 29 games – and an even better one on their bank balance. Cole was hot news in football and Newcastle swooped to buy him for £1.75 million as the player proved that not only could he continue to score goals at a higher level, he could also improve his striking rate. At St James' Park he bagged 12 from 12 in what was left of the 1992–93 season.

Starting from scratch in the 1993–94 season he scored a remarkable 34 from 40 League matches. Anything not tidied up in the six-yard box was buried by Cole, a player with phenomenal short-distance speed and a ruthless instinct for goals. If Newcastle were going to challenge seriously for the

Premiership title, then Cole seemed to be their main weapon. But after nine goals in 18 games Kevin Keegan sensationally sold him to arch-rivals Manchester United for £7 million in January 1995. The income was of little comfort to distraught Newcastle fans.

At Old Trafford Alex Ferguson carefully played-in Cole and he managed 12 goals in what remained of the 1994–95 season, but only 11 in 34 appearances during the next year. Suddenly his confidence seemed to have gone, and chances that he would once have buried in his sleep were being ballooned.

Ferguson knows, however, that a prolific goalscorer does not become bad overnight and with careful support Cole has returned to form. He has become deadly again around the six-yard box; his reading of the game is growing match by match and he has made an invaluable contribution to the United cause.

Cole's international experience may be limited but he is undoubtedly one of the form strikers in the English game. He is a player who has shown he can cope with pressure and that he won't let a bad run get him down. Better still for England, he is something of an unknown package – international opponents will not have faced him before, providing a dangerous element of surprise. France '98 could be the start of something special for Andy Cole.

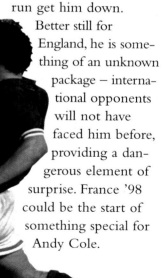

Rio Ferdinand

Club: West Ham
Previous clubs: none
Height: 6'2"
Born: 7 November 1978
International debut: v Cameroon (sub) 2-0 (Wembley) 15 November 1997

'If I could be half as good as Bobby Moore, and achieve half as much, it will have all been worth it – but at the same time I have to be my own person.'

After a false start when he was called up to the England squad for the game against Moldova, and then left out for disciplinary reasons, Rio Ferdinand took the lesson on board, vowed to mend his ways and won his first cap against Cameroon.

Even in the fast-moving world of professional football, Ferdinand's rise has been meteoric. Until the 1997–98 season he was yet to complete a full programme of first-team football, but in only a handful of games had made a massive impression.

Harry Redknapp, his manager at West Ham, knew immediately he had a player of immense confidence; comfortable on the ball and willing to join the attack from deep positions. The praise from rivals, including cousin Les Ferdinand at Tottenham, was equally fulsome.

Ferdinand's cause has been helped by Hoddle's willingness to bring on youngsters, to invite the special talents in the game to England training sessions so that they can have a glimpse of an international life, and so that they can get comfortable with it should their day come.

The first time Ferdinand was called up was during England's Euro '96 campaign and at a stage in his career when he had completed just one full match for West Ham. When the letter arrived with the three lions stamp, Ferdinand read it and thought there had to be some mistake. It was only when he went through it a second time that it sunk in – he was asked to join the full England squad for training.

Ferdinand is an engaging mix of self-confidence and naivety. On top of that he has a healthy respect for the past, regrets that he never saw Bobby Moore play for West Ham, takes on board with pride that he has been compared with England's World Cup captain, and then disarmingly admits that some of the mates with whom he used to play Sunday football are better players than he is.

There is no doubt that he is a player born into the job. His skill is such that, although a relative novice in the Premier League, he has the cool to handle the tense situations and refuses to be intimidated by the physical stuff.

His big chance came when Aston Villa's Gareth Southgate damaged an ankle in the Cameroon match and Ferdinand ran out on to the pitch to become, at the time, England's third youngest full international this century.

Ferdinand stands at the front of the England youth movement, a player to carry England into the new century.

Tim Flowers

Club: Blackburn Rovers
Previous clubs: Southampton, Wolverhampton Wanderers
Height: 6'2"
Born: 3 February 1967
International debut: v Brazil 1-1 (Washington DC) 13 June 1993

'I have to work harder than most to get where I am. I am not a natural with great God-given talents like Gordon Banks and Peter Shilton.'

Up, down and around, Tim Flowers is proof that the right work ethic along with the right attitude can bring its rewards.

The battle to join the top three England goalkeepers has been intense. David Seaman is clearly the No. 1, but behind him Nigel Martyn has been in favour and out, but is now back again and David James has slipped out of the rankings, but Tim Flowers has hung on in there.

Flowers started his goalkeeping career with Wolves, then moved to Southampton where he conceded five goals in his first game and fractured a cheekbone in the next. He was bought by Blackburn Rovers for £2 million in November 1993.

Ewood Park has been a happy home. He won a Premiership title with the club and has gone from strength to strength — the only blot on the landscape is the occasional very public howler that has been replayed and analysed to the point of no return.

On that score goalkeepers are in a league of their own, because nobody forgets their errors — not even when the man in the No. 1 shirt has a reasonable case for his defence. Remember that Stan Collymore goal for Liverpool against Blackburn? A weak shot heading for the arms of Flowers hit a divot and took an unreal bounce over his shoulder into the net, leaving Collymore to acknowledge the goal almost apologetically.

There was another one like that in late December 1997, when former team-mate Paul Warhurst scored a crazy goal for Crystal Palace with a header that took a bizarre bounce and again reared up over Flowers' shoulder. It says a great deal about his temperament that he has not crept into Ewood Park at night and dug up the pitch. As for the talent that makes him an England goalkeeper — the proof is in the breathtaking stops he makes, too numerous to be recounted in specific detail.

As a youngster, Flowers supported Coventry City and wanted to be a centre-forward, but his failure to trap the ball led him to a place between the posts where he could make a worthwhile contribution.

'I can only try to impress by all I do at Blackburn and that's why I go out on the training pitch and work two or three hours a day, just to try to be at my best and stay that way,' he says.

Ray Harford, his former manager at Blackburn, says: 'He is very self-critical, but that's no bad thing. He's also very chirpy about most things. If Tim makes errors he accepts them, will work out in his own mind what went wrong and why — then he'll look forward.'

It is significant that Blackburn have done so much better when Flowers has been on top of his game. He gives them a confidence that can't be bought — a valuable commodity at all times, but possibly priceless for England in a World Cup campaign.

Paul Gascoigne

Club: Glasgow Rangers
Previous clubs: Lazio, Tottenham, Newcastle
Height: 5'10"
Born: 27 May 1967
International debut: v Denmark (sub) 1-0
(Wembley) 14 September 1988

'I wish I could be a year younger – but if I keep my fitness then hopefully we can all have a nice time at the World Cup.'

The clown prince of English football burst on to the scene with his home-town club Newcastle United back in 1985 and has hardly been out of the spotlight since. A footballing genius who has been compared with George Best, Gascoigne has spent much of his career battling with a self-destructive streak that would have ruined many a lesser talent.

He was adored at St James' Park and played 106 matches for the club, scoring 22 goals, before joining Tottenham in 1988 for £2 million. Ironically, he made his debut with the London club at Newcastle in a 2-2 draw in September 1988. Eleven days later he made his first England appearance.

A creative midfield player with the pace and close control to prise open the most limpet-like defences, Gascoigne went to the World Cup in Italy in 1990 and became a global star – wearing his heart on his sleeve as England reached the semi-finals. There were tears when Gascoigne was booked during the match, which meant that even if England had won, he would have been forced to miss the Final.

Back with Tottenham, he was in the side that reached the 1991 FA Cup Final, but he damaged cruciate knee ligaments in the opening minutes and was carried off. The injury put him out of football for 16 months. Three knee operations later, Gascoigne was fit and ready to play again – this time in Italy for Lazio, who had paid £5.5 million for his services.

More bad luck was waiting around the corner, though. In April 1994 he broke a leg in training and was out of action for a year. Glasgow Rangers brought him back to Britain at the start of the 1995–96 season and he became a key figure in helping the side to an eighth consecutive Scottish League title.

With that success came the rejuvenation of his international career and he was to spearhead England's march to the semi-finals of Euro '96, his finest hour and a half coming in the 4-1 thrashing of Holland in the group stage. On that Wembley night Gascoigne was sensational – full of energy and deft touches as he set up England for one of their best victories of modern times.

This was no swansong, however, for Gascoigne was to be an essential part of Glenn Hoddle's plans for the England World Cup qualifying campaign. Older, wiser, but still the joker in the pack, he was often castigated in the press for his excesses, but it is a difficult balancing act because a subdued Gascoigne off the pitch is subdued on it.

This will almost certainly be his last World Cup and Gascoigne will feel that after the tears of his previous international escapades, the time has come for the clown of English football to have the last laugh.

Andy Hinchcliffe

Club: Sheffield Wednesday
Previous clubs: Everton, Manchester City
Height: 5'10"
Born: 5 February 1969
International debut: v Moldova 3-0
(Chisinau) 1 September 1996

'I've always enjoyed my football but I've never been immersed in it — I want to play with a smile on my face rather than be so wound up.'

A first cap won in demanding circumstances — England's opening World Cup qualifying match in Group 2 — singled Andy Hinchcliffe out as a man who could cope with the pressures of international football.

Hinchcliffe is now an attacking left-back with Sheffield Wednesday, and a man who will quietly get over any problems strewn in his path. He had to battle with David Unsworth for a place at Everton, and then suffered a knee ligament injury which put him out of action for nine months. But rather than buckle, Hinchcliffe gritted his teeth and got on with it, winning back his Everton place. Heartened by the England management's approach — they kept in touch with him throughout his nine-month lay-off — he returned as quietly determined as ever.

Hinchcliffe is a rarity in football; a man with more O levels than fingers, and an academic future beckoned when he was at William Hulme School in Manchester. As he considered higher education, Manchester City came in and offered him the chance to join them.

Realizing that he could return to studying later, Hinchcliffe decided to give it a go and quickly became a regular in the side before Everton moved in for him in July 1990, spending £800,000 to secure his services.

Life at Everton was eventful — often for the wrong reasons — but Hinchcliffe at least enjoyed the glory of the club's 1995 FA Cup triumph when they beat Manchester United 1-0 in the Final.

Hinchcliffe was a keen cricketer at school, where he played against Mike Atherton and John Crawley — then at Manchester Grammar School — and he also developed a passion for lacrosse. Shy to such an extent that when he has won Man of the Match awards in the past he has delegated other players to collect the prize on his behalf, Hinchcliffe is very much the modern player, aware that he needs to be very fit and very fast. The responsibility of that first England game did not overawe him and a 3-0 win in Moldova, followed two months later by a 2-0 victory in Georgia, suggests that he is more than capable of doing a good job.

The rivalry for the England left-back berth is intense, with those in competition for it — including Graeme Le Saux and Philip Neville — knowing that it is not just about defending, but also attacking at speed and delivering good crosses. Hinchcliffe might shun the spotlight, but he could be heading for a major part in England's World Cup finals campaign.

Paul Ince

Club: Liverpool
Previous clubs: Inter Milan, Manchester United, West Ham
Height: 5'10"
Born: 21 October 1967
International debut: v Spain 0-1 (Santander) 9 September 1992

'It annoys me when people say that Incey is going to be the anchor man for England – I like to express myself. To me "anchor" sounds like a player who has got a limited talent.'

For anchor, substitute motor, heart and soul. Anyone who witnessed Ince's performance for England in Rome last October could be in no doubt that this man could get run over by a steamroller and still get up and play his heart out. Nicknamed 'The Gov'nor' he lives up to the image. In Rome, for the crucial World Cup qualifying match with Italy, he split his head open in the first half and had to leave the pitch, but he was soon patched up and back out there bossing the troops, his shirt stained red with blood.

Ince is the sort of leader who doesn't expect people to do something he wouldn't do himself. Hard and combative, he mixes aggression with subtle skills and he certainly creates a sense of 'all for one and one for all'.

His career started at West Ham in 1981, where he was an associated schoolboy accepted on to the YTS scheme. After four years he signed professional terms and in 1986 he made his debut for the club. He scored on his full debut against Southampton and became the darling of Upton Park ... until he posed for a picture in a Manchester United shirt before he had signed for the team.

The deal in 1989 was for £800,000 plus £5,000 for every game played in the United firsts over the next two years. He soon settled and was central to United's re-emergence as the powerhouse of English football, winning the FA Cup in 1990, the Cup Winners' Cup in 1991, two Premiership titles and a further FA Cup in 1994.

Meanwhile his England career was up and running. Ince became an automatic choice with Terry Venables and then his successor, Glenn Hoddle, after the end of the Graham Taylor era. When he was handed the captain's armband by Taylor for a game against the USA in Boston back in 1993, he became the first black player to lead England.

Then in June 1995, Ince moved from United to Inter Milan for £7.5 million, but his early days in Italy were a severe culture shock. He was applauded for speaking out against racist chants on the terraces, but struggled to come to terms with the Italian way of playing.

The arrival of Roy Hodgson as coach in place of Ottavio Bianchi rejuvenated him, earned an extension to his Inter contract and lifted the club. Such was his influence that despite repeated rumours that he and his family were having trouble settling there, Inter rejected an offer of £6.5 million for him from Arsenal in late 1995.

Eventually, with Ince keen to return home, Inter sold him to Liverpool for £4.2 million in July 1997, when Manchester United did not follow up their buy-back option from the original deal. Liverpool were convinced that Ince still had the competitive edge and that he had matured – no longer the hard-man, now the sophisticated, iron-willed competitor. Every team needs one.

Graeme Le Saux

Club: Chelsea
Previous clubs: Blackburn Rovers, Chelsea
Height: 5'10"
Born: 17 October 1968
International debut: v Denmark (sub) 1-0
(Wembley) 9 March 1994

'England is very important to me, I have tried to look at it as a reward for playing well and consistently for my club.'

It was always going to be a battle between Le boys of the Channel Isles to see who was going to be the first to win a full England cap. In one corner stood the favourite, Matt Le Tissier – in the other, Graeme Le Saux.

In the end it was Le Saux who won, picked to start against Denmark in 1994, and it was Le Tissier who came second by a short head, coming on as a substitute for his first cap in the same match. For Jersey and Guernsey to have sourced two England players in the same international was remarkable. For Le Saux, wearing

England colours and rampaging down the wing is second nature and he was sorely missed when a broken ankle forced him out of England's 1996 campaign.

Le Saux is one of football's more fascinating characters because he does not conform in any way to the stereotypical image of a footballer. Here is a man who stands out in the changing room because he reads *The Guardian*. Time off means a visit to a museum or an art gallery, while his musical preferences are not the standard fare of Celine Dion, Meat Loaf or Oasis – but something far more esoteric.

He was discovered by Chelsea playing for St Pauls in Jersey and made his top-flight debut on Boxing Day in 1989. Although he scored in this

match, and his career began to take off at Stamford Bridge, he only progressed so far. Switched between midfield and defence and caught in the crossfire of managerial changes, Le Saux realized he was going stale. His game suffered and eventually he was sold to Blackburn Rovers for £750,000. Today that looks like one of the greatest buys of all time. Le Saux rediscovered his zest for the game, was switched to the back and, with Kenny Dalglish at the helm, Rovers went on to win the Premiership title. Heady days indeed.

The following season, however, Blackburn made a dog's dinner of their European Champions' League campaign, which came to a head when Le Saux and team-mate David Batty ended up fighting on the pitch during the game against Moscow Spartak. It was the beginning of the end for Le Saux at Blackburn.

Injury curtailed much of his 1995–96 season, Dalglish left the club and in the end Le Saux asked for a transfer. Blackburn priced him at £7.5 million but finally accepted an offer of £5 million from Chelsea – who were big enough to admit that they should never have sold him in the first place.

Le Saux arrived back in London, determined to win honours with the club and to rebuild his England career. So far, so good for the defender who can boast that he has scored a goal for his country against Brazil. A repeat in France would do nicely.

Nigel Martyn

Club: Leeds United
Previous clubs: Crystal Palace, Bristol Rovers
Height: 6'2"
Born: 11 August 1966
International debut: v CIS (sub) 2-2
(Moscow) 29 April 1992

'Being a goalkeeper is not a bit like anything else but I like my job – I suppose I am a bit of a perfectionist but as a goalkeeper you have to be.'

George Graham signed David Seaman for Arsenal back in 1990 and had no doubts that he was the best goalkeeper in the English game – but at that point he did not know too much about Cornishman, Nigel Martyn.

The years passed, football fortunes ebbed and flowed and in September 1996 Graham found himself hired as manager at Leeds United, inheriting a squad that contained Martyn. Graham was quickly won over. If

Seaman was the best, then Martyn came a close second.

The record book backs Graham to the hilt. During the 1996–97 season Martyn was the king of the clean sheets, keeping 19. Week after week he produced breathtaking stops and was rewarded by the Leeds supporters who made him their Player of the Year.

Graham was not far behind the fans with his praise, constantly and publicly wondering why his goalkeeper had not been recruited to the England cause. Martyn, the first £1 million goalkeeper in British football when he was signed by Steve Coppell for Crystal Palace in November 1989, won three caps while at the South London club. As Palace did their best impression of a lift – going up meant they were always coming down – so Martyn's England chances faded.

Martyn made his England debut in April 1992, replacing Chris Woods in Moscow for a game against the CIS and then starting against Hungary two weeks later. One year on he had the distinction of being the first England goalkeeper to play a full international indoors and on grass – when England played Germany in Detroit during the US Cup.

He then went down the pecking order until his form with Leeds – reinforced by Graham's words and the opinions of supporters, both from Leeds and from clubs thwarted by Martyn – led to a rethink. Martyn won his fourth cap, his first as a Leeds player, in May 1997 when England beat South Africa 2-1 at Old Trafford. He was then in goal for the Wembley international against Cameroon.

Martyn, a quiet and unassuming character off the field, says that the move to Leeds had been the tonic his game needed and that this, along with the challenge of winning over a new set of fans, made him a better goalkeeper than when he first wore an England shirt. His move away from Palace broke the British transfer fee record for a goalkeeper for a second time when Leeds paid £2.25 million for his services.

It is reassuring for England to know that in Martyn they have a man who thrives on responsibility, a man who rises to the challenge of pressure with calm, confidence and no little skill.

Steve McManaman

Club: Liverpool
Previous clubs: none
Height: 6'0"
Born: 11 February 1972
International debut: v Nigeria (sub) 1-0 (Wembley) 16 November 1994

'Goalscoring is a major thing missing from my game but there are other parts I have to improve – defending, heading – even the good things can be improved. I see people dribbling and I feel I can learn off them.'

McManaman is one of those enigmas of the game. The type that haunts every manager, and a player England coach Glenn Hoddle will appreciate because he too, in his playing prime, was an enigma. He will see something of himself in the vastly talented Liverpool winger.

Hoddle could destroy any side in the world with his passing and his vision, and the same is true of Steve McManaman, who is a world-beater on a good day but has not yet produced consistently on the world stage. He can run the length of the field with the ball at his feet, seemingly attached to it by a piece of string – and score stupendous goals. The problem is finding out exactly what role he should play. McManaman has proved at club level that he is a player with a big-match temperament and his role there, as a roving midfielder, suits him fine. But he knows that such freedom comes with a price tag. He has to be responsible, roll up his sleeves and get back and defend when needed.

The lack of goals, six or seven a season since he became a Liverpool regular back in 1991–92, troubles him. McManaman says it is because he is looking to make the telling pass to his forwards, that he does not have that centre-forward's ruthless streak, to get the ball and head for goal.

For England, his strength is the space he makes with his runs, sucking in defenders, and that is an aspect that Hoddle would like him to work on, along with a sharper touch to his game in the last third of the field. To provide for the forwards is his main function and Hoddle believes if he does that, then the goals will come.

An Everton fan who was picked up by Liverpool, McManaman came through the ranks at Anfield and won England Youth and Under-21 caps. Last summer with Simon Fuller, the former manager of the Spice Girls pop group, acting for him, he was rumoured to be on the verge of a £12 million move to Barcelona, but there was no deal.

Off the field McManaman, a former North-west Schools' cross-country champion, is very much the thinking footballer. He has a column in *The Times* and although a player actively involved in the game faces restrictions, he has not been afraid to voice his opinions.

While Hoddle knows what he wants from McManaman, the problem remains getting him to deliver. The fact that he can and does with Liverpool is as frustrating as it is enticing, but then he just might be the unpredictable wild-card that England need in France.

Gary Neville

Club: Manchester United
Previous clubs: none
Height: 5'10"
Born: 18 February 1975
International debut: v Japan 2-1 (Wembley) 3 June 1995

'As far as I'm concerned everything has happened so quickly. You can't always comprehend what is going on, but this is all I have ever wanted to do.'

When the going gets tough and Glenn Hoddle can only take 22 players with him to the finals in France, the good old utility player will come into his own – and that should benefit Gary Neville.

A tried and trusted international with England, Neville has slotted easily into the defence and taken to the demands of international football as if he has always been playing at that level. He is as accomplished on the right flank as he is switching to the middle.

This is a job he has done at Manchester United when Gary Pallister has been injured, and he has played as if to the manner born. A hard-tackling player who is also quick, Neville can naturally take the attack down the right. This, along with his ability to deliver a long throw-in – an underrated talent – makes him a multi-purpose player and a valuable commodity in any team.

Two years older than brother Philip, Gary was the first to show at Old Trafford and the first to make it to the full England team – but these are brothers determined to help each other out, not become embroiled in a battle to be king boy in the family.

It is an attitude borne out by Gary's reaction to a booking in Euro '96 which left him as a spectator when England played Germany in the semi-final. Angry with himself, but accepting he was at fault, Gary said that what happened to him did not matter, it was all about England winning through to the Final.

The Neville brothers are multi-talented when it comes to sport. Philip was wooed by Lancashire County Cricket Club, and for a while they both played in the same Bury Under-14 side. Once, when facing Rochdale, Philip scored a century and then Gary took all ten wickets as Bury won at a canter.

The Alex Ferguson philosophy to give youth a chance has certainly been readily embraced by Gary, but then as a Manchester United fan since before he can remember, and as a young man not attracted by the bright lights of the nightclub, he is the ideal person to be put in such a position. He will take to heart Ferguson's instruction to go out and play without abusing his freedom.

Such is the family strength of the Nevilles that even though Gary has recently bought his own home, more often than not he can be found back at the family semi-detached home, enjoying his mother's cooking and the rest of the family's company.

Neville has already won more than 20 caps and with a bit of luck, skill and determination, he could well go on to become one of England's leading cap-winners. And if it happens Gary will say it was all down to his family, his club team-mates and his England colleagues – luckily he is not so generous on the pitch.

Philip Neville

Club: Manchester United
Previous clubs: none
Height: 5'10"
Born: 21 January 1977
International debut: v China 3-0
(Beijing) 23 May 1996

'I've been nervous just watching England and the National Anthem has been sung so loud it has made the hairs on the back of my neck stand up.'

Not since the Charltons – Bobby and Jack – have England played brothers in the same side. Gary and Philip Neville, both defenders, are following a famous act ... and with some style.

Philip is the younger of the two and won his first full international cap when he was picked to face China back in 1996. But such is the relationship between them that it is not about who is first, it is about helping each other to success. And they come from some sporting family. While Gary and Philip have made their way through the ranks at Old Trafford – Gary was first to be picked for the first team – their sister Tracey has been winning England honours at netball.

The Neville brothers have built up quite a reputation as a double-act. When with England they room together and some observers swear that when one of them is injured the other, though fully fit, has also struggled.

They have played with the same clubs since they first turned out for Sunday youth teams, and have progressed to higher levels – yet Phil might easily have changed direction and played professional cricket. He was picked to play for Lancashire seconds when only 15 and it took the lure of Old Trafford to make him change direction. He has England cricket caps at Under-14 and Under-15 age groups and says that had United not made him feel so welcome, he might still be playing the summer game for a living.

The Nevilles are famed for their sensible living – both have a dislike of nightclubs and would rather have a mug of cocoa than a bottle of beer –

and in that sense they are dream boys for United boss Alex Ferguson.

Philip's rise has been spectacular. He had played just twice for United prior to the start of the 1995–96 season, but his strength and domination in the air, allied to tough tackling, won him the United right-back spot from brother Gary. That freed the older Neville to play a utility role.

Success has come at United, Phil playing an important part in the double-winning side of 1996. And while the Neville brothers have become superstars and big earners, their feet have remained so firmly on the ground that for a long while they preferred to stay at home, sharing a room in their parents' semi-detached house.

Phil admits that United's policy of playing youngsters if they are good enough has helped his career enormously, and says that the atmosphere at the club, where the seasoned professionals are willing to help and encourage the juniors, has played a big part in their success.

United in Manchester, brothers-in-arms for England, the Nevilles experienced near-glory with England in Euro '96 and would like to do better in France '98.

Michael Owen

Club: Liverpool
Previous clubs: none
Height: 5'8"
Born: 14 December 1979
International debut: v Chile 0-2 (Wembley)
10 February 1998

'I feel confident enough in my own ability to do well – I don't think age comes into it. If you are good enough, you are old enough.'

Could Michael Owen be the ace in Hoddle's pack? So far the Liverpool youngster has displayed a maturity well beyond his years and a nose for goal that would be the envy of the most experienced and successful of the Premiership goal-winners. It is this ability that has put him in the frame to become England's youngest player in the World Cup finals, and as far as future opponents are concerned, his skills are far more of a threat than the element of surprise he brings to the England team. Give this young man a sight of goal and he'll go for it.

Owen has been the wonder-boy of the 1997–98 season, showing that whatever the level, he can not only play, he can also be a star. He has been touted as something special from the word go, when he broke Ian Rush's scoring record for Deeside School, hitting 97 in a 42-match season – 25 more than the Liverpool legend managed in his time.

The son of a former Everton player, Owen was the subject of a mad rush from various clubs – including Arsenal and Manchester United – all wanting to sign him. The Anfield Reds won. By the time he was 15, Owen had signed his first kit deal and, at 17, Liverpool gave him a five-year contract worth £2.5 million. Hot property, big pressure – not that you would guess this from Owen's quiet but determined demeanour.

Playing for Liverpool meant finding a place in a side that has Robbie Fowler and Karlheinz Riedle also wanting to start every match, but was Owen fazed by this? Not one bit. Liverpool manager Roy Evans had no hesitation in handing him a first-team squad shirt – No. 18 – and Owen has proved himself worthy of it.

He made his debut towards the end of the 1996–97 season, and he became Liverpool's second youngest first-team player. He marked that occasion, against Wimbledon, with a goal after 17 minutes of action, and has made a habit of scoring ever since.

He has lived up to his reputation on the pitch. 'He's a gem,' says Steve Heighway, the Anfield Youth Development Officer. 'He's very popular with the other lads and he is very strong mentally as well as being technically gifted. I've no doubts about him – he just needs to carry on as he has been.'

His strengths are his pace and his speed of reaction. On top of this, he is a two-footed player and despite being small, he will not be intimidated. Owen plays down the middle and, unusually for that position, likes to take on defenders. He has the ability and pace to run at them with the ball. Add this to the knack of finding space and exquisite timing when it comes to making a run from deep, and you have a player who really is a handful for the opposition. Comparisons with the Brazilian Ronaldo are not overkill.

Owen has been capped by England at Under-16, -18, -20 and -21 levels. He skippered the Under-18 side but suffered the one black moment of his career when he was sent off in a draw with Yugoslavia. This has been put down to the impudence of youth. It is what he learned from it that counts. For the time being, Hoddle is prepared to let Owen find his feet in his own time – and the way it has gone so far, that will be double-quick. The rest of the world might just be caught napping by this youngster.

Jamie Redknapp

Club: Liverpool
Previous clubs: Bournemouth
Height: 6'0"
Born: 25 June 1973
International debut: v Colombia 0-0
(Wembley) 6 September 1995

'Football is my life, it always has been. I talk to my Dad every day without fail and 99.9 per cent of the conversation is about football. Some people might think that's shallow but nothing else interests me.'

A schoolboy with Tottenham Hotspur, it was at Bournemouth that Jamie Redknapp cut his teeth as a professional, and it only took a few matches for the rest of the game to know about his prodigious talents. But then, having Harry Redknapp, the West Ham manager, as his father, it was certain he would be talked about in footballing circles.

It was Liverpool and Kenny Dalglish who, in 1990, came up with £350,000 to buy the then 17-year-old from Bournemouth; and at Anfield his abilities have matured nicely. He now has a reputation as one of the best passers of the ball in the modern game.

Glenn Hoddle, the England coach, is a fan and sees Redknapp as the ideal sweeper because of his ability to hit long searching passes. Indeed, Redknapp had a significant impact on England's Euro '96 campaign when called on as a substitute against Scotland, transforming the match with his deft touches. But Redknapp has been cursed by injury. A knock later in that same Scotland match kept him out for the rest of the competition and then, playing against South Africa in the summer of 1997, he suffered another blow. As a result, international appearances have been restricted, but he is still very much in mind and he has been invited to train with England even when not in serious contention for a place back in the side.

Life at Liverpool with fellow soul mates Steve McManaman, Robbie Fowler and Jason McAteer has not been as rosy as it should have been. These are four supremely talented footballers playing for a Liverpool team weighed down by expectations founded on past glories. When the team has not performed, Redknapp and Co. have been the first to take the flak.

Redknapp's image as one of football's glamour boys does not help. Here is a man who is a regular pull-out poster in teenage girls' magazines; here is a man who admits to enjoying holidays with the lads; here is a man who, by being himself, ends up as envy's target.

The truth is that Redknapp cares passionately, can often be found training on a day off back at the ground, working hard in the company of McManaman, Fowler and McAteer. He knows that for all the talent and self-belief, more is needed.

It has been a struggle of late for Redknapp, but when Terry Venables, the former England coach, lumped Redknapp and David Beckham together as England's two best prospects, he wasn't making a prediction, he was commenting on the evidence before his experienced eye. England needs both of them.

Paul Scholes

Club: Manchester United
Previous clubs: none
Height: 5'7"
Born: 16 November 1974
International debut: v South Africa (sub) 2-1 (Old Trafford) 24 May 1997

'You have to feel confident when you play for England, there's no point staying in your shell, you've got to express yourself. As I play more and more games I feel increasingly confident.'

The day before his 23rd birthday Paul Scholes made his third England start, scored a sensational goal against Cameroon and had Glenn Hoddle, the England manager, proclaiming him to be the potential jewel in the nation's footballing crown. Not bad for an asthma sufferer who earned a reputation for the wrong things whilst a young teenager playing with Rochdale Boys. Told that he should be defending more, Scholes saw red and walked out. At the time he was with Manchester United's School of Excellence and nothing could tempt him back.

On the plus side, he had left behind memories of a player with tremendous vision and the ability to make things happen. United manager Alex Ferguson has been suitably impressed and compared him with Kenny Dalglish. Living up to those expectations is hard – but the reality harder still. At Old Trafford Scholes has, to some extent, come in for Eric Cantona, who retired from the game in 1997. By going, Cantona was thought to have left a void that could not be filled. Yet Scholes has effortlessly taken over, and where Cantona was the strutting master of all he surveyed, Scholes is the sniping destroyer.

Happy to boss his elders, Scholes is an all-action player, forever demanding the ball, forever prompting his team on. He is a potent substitute, able to come into the thick of the action, pick up on the tempo and dictate the shape of the match to come. A look at his record shows just how useful he has been – valuable goals all down the line, whatever the company. Much of United's success has been founded on touches of Scholes' magic.

Coaches see him as their dream player; he is willing to work hard, is physically and mentally tough, is unaffected by the beckoning limelight and is a team player with the virtuoso's touch. Even the non-United fans, prejudiced by envy, have warmed to him. Evidence of this can be seen in the reaction to England's display against Cameroon. A crowd that had been singing 'Stand up if you hate Man U', rose *en masse* to applaud and cheer Scholes as he trotted past them, replaced by Chris Sutton with ten minutes of the match remaining.

Scholes is the model professional, a young man capable of turning a fleeting chance into an opportunity for life. At Manchester United you either make the grade quickly or disappear even faster. Scholes has ensured he will be around for years to come. He has come into the reckoning late on and with what is, in truth, limited experience. That he has risen to the challenge so well fills England with confidence.

David Seaman

Club: Arsenal
Previous clubs: QPR, Birmingham, Peterborough, Leeds United
Height: 6'4"
Born: 19 September 1963
International debut: v Saudi Arabia 1-1 (Riyadh) 16 November 1988

'Goalkeeping is an art, it's about angles, space and timing. Bravery comes into it and you need to be able to make up your mind.'

Behind every good defence stands an even better goalkeeper and in David Seaman England have one of the best.

To wear the No. 1 shirt for England is to join a club where the previous incumbents have gone on to win caps galore – look at Gordon Banks with his 73 caps, Ray Clemence with 61 and Peter Shilton with 125.

Set against these three, Seaman's haul is not so impressive, but then he had to fight his way past Chris Woods, the Sheffield Wednesday goalkeeper, who had collected 43 caps. Seaman managed that at the start of the 1993–94 season and since then England have looked oddly vulnerable whenever he has been unavailable.

The only match they lost during the World Cup qualifiers was against Italy at Wembley, on a night when Seaman was absent. That apart, only one other goal was conceded during qualifying and the likes of Sol Campbell, Gareth Southgate, Tony Adams and Gary Neville seemed to grow an inch taller and run with a swagger because they knew Seaman was behind them.

Seaman certainly made his mark in Euro '96, when he saved a penalty against Scotland and was on top form to deny Spain by means of a penalty shoot-out in their quarter-final. He was not so lucky in the

semi-final against Germany but it was not through lack of research and thought. Laid back though he appears, Seaman – who enjoys nothing better than a day spent on a river bank, rod in hand – spends much of his time thinking about strikers and the way they take penalties; whether they blast them; whether they prefer to go left or right; whether they have a quirky run-up.

Seaman was born in Rotherham in September 1963 and signed on as an apprentice with Leeds United in September 1981. He never got to play a first-team game for the Yorkshire club. Sold to Peterborough for £4,000, he increased his value 25-fold after playing 91 League matches for the club.

Birmingham was his next port of call, signed for £100,000 in October 1984. He spent two seasons there before being bought for £225,000 by Queens Park Rangers. The move to Loftus Road raised his profile and it was during his time there that he was capped by England for the first time. When Arsenal needed a new goalkeeper for the 1990–91 season, they reached for the chequebook and bought Seaman for £1.3 million.

He had an incredible first season at Highbury. Arsenal won the title, lost just one match all season and conceded a miserly 18 goals in 38 matches. To put that in even sharper perspective, second-placed Liverpool and third-placed Crystal Palace leaked 40 and 41 goals respectively.

For England he is a rock. The laid-back giant revelling in his job; an inspiration to his team-mates, to the fans and to every young boy who dreams of being a goalie.

Alan Shearer

Club: Newcastle United
Previous Clubs: Blackburn Rovers, Southampton
Height: 5'11"
Born: 13 August 1970
International debut: v France 2-0 (scored) (Wembley) 19 February 1992

'The England team are on a high at the moment, they have been since before Euro '96 and have carried on from there under Glenn Hoddle.'

The statistics say it all – Alan Shearer is the first man to score more than 30 goals in three consecutive seasons in the top flight since the 1930s. If it wasn't for an ankle injury he would have been odds-on to have done it again in the 1997–98 season.

In days of sky-high transfer fees, at least Shearer – at a British record £15 million – looks like value for money. At Newcastle he had scored 25 goals in 31 games; that breaks down as one every game and 24 minutes.

He has a reputation as a quick healer – prior to Euro '96 he missed the end of the season with Blackburn to have a groin operation, but even so he was back for England by the start of the Championship and quickly put behind him a poor run for his country by scoring five goals in five games as England reached the semi-finals.

Shearer is the complete striker: strong, quick, brave and instinctive. Many countries would have built their team around him, but England are a touch more circumspect and have adjusted to his absence with solid pragmatism and no little flair. Having him back, however, will be a huge bonus and lift a squad already believing it can win the World Cup.

Shearer started out as a trainee with Southampton, graduated to the first team and scored 23 goals in 118 games. Then Blackburn, just promoted to the Premiership, bought him at the start of the 1992–93 season for what was at the time a staggering £3.6 million. It was money well spent as the club consolidated their new-found position in their first two seasons, then won the title in the next. Shearer was to score 122 goals in 138 matches for Rovers and form a sparkling partnership with Chris Sutton.

The striker everybody wanted, Manchester United as keen as anyone, Shearer bowed to the sentimental pull of his roots, to join Newcastle United after Euro '96 and insisted that he should wear the club's famous No. 9 shirt.

Shearer was injured in August 1997 in a preseason tournament – a bitter loss for Newcastle, who had just agreed to sell Shearer's striking partner, Les Ferdinand, to Spurs. As a result, Newcastle's season was not all plain sailing. But a fit Shearer, for both Newcastle and England, is a prospect to terrify defences around the world.

Teddy Sheringham

Club: Manchester United
Previous clubs: Tottenham, Nottingham Forest, Millwall
Height: 6'0"
Born: 2 April 1966
International debut: v Poland 1-1
(Chorzow) 29 May 1993

'You have got to have something extra. You have got to understand the way international opposition play and the methods they have for stopping you.'

There is no dispute that Alan Shearer is England's No. 1 striker. The problem and the permutations come with finding a man to play alongside him; a player who can bring out the best from the Newcastle man; a player to hold the ball up and a player to make his own goalscoring contribution.

Step forward Teddy Sheringham. There has been an added pressure on England strikers brought about by Shearer's injury, but Sheringham, much admired by Glenn Hoddle, has risen to the challenge. Now at an age when what he knows is as important as how fast he can run, Sheringham has proved his worth by scoring wherever he has played his football.

He started out as an apprentice with Millwall, making his first appearance in the 1983–84 season when he scored one goal in seven matches. It was a time when the South London side were on the up and Sheringham formed a mighty partnership with Tony Cascarino – the Republic of Ireland striker. Both men scored goals galore as Millwall topped the Second Division in 1988 and went on to enjoy one good season in the top flight – the club's first appearance at that level – before being relegated in 1989–90. One more season in the old Second Division and Sheringham showed that he had learned a thing or two as he scored a phenomenal 33 goals in 46 matches.

Nottingham Forest, in need of a sharp striker, paid £2 million for him and in one season at the City Ground,

Sheringham scored at the rate of one goal every three games. But homesickness set in and after just three matches for Forest in his second season, he was off again – back to London and to Tottenham Hotspur. Forest made a small profit, selling him for £2.1 million.

Good strikers will always score goals, irrespective of the company they are keeping, and Sheringham passed this test with flying colours. In 38 games in his first season with Spurs he scored 21 goals. An injury-ravaged 1993–94 still produced 14 goals in 19 matches and then the following year he scored another 18.

When Eric Cantona left Manchester United in the summer of 1997, it became clear that Alex Ferguson would want a tried-and-trusted replacement. Sheringham, at £3.5 million, was the man – even if the news did come as a surprise to him.

The Old Trafford environment and the quality of their play can only help to make Sheringham a better player; to be the perfect foil to Shearer but have his own sharp goalscoring edge. Sheringham has shown that he is good enough for the job.

Gareth Southgate

Club: Aston Villa
Previous clubs: Crystal Palace
Height: 6'0"
Born: 30 September 1970
International debut: v Portugal (sub) 1-1
(Wembley) 12 December 1995

'I'm sure people will always say I was the idiot who missed the penalty, but I've got enough time in my career to do other things, make people remember me in other ways.'

Southgate and *that* penalty miss in the 1996 Euro Championship will long be an enduring football image. Unlike the World Cup in 1990, when Stuart Pearce and Chris Waddle missed in a semi-final shoot-out, Southgate was the sole sufferer – there was no one to share the guilt on that balmy June night. Yet his appearance in Euro '96 was testament to what can be achieved by an ambitious player. He had only broken into the England squad six months earlier, but here he was not just a part of Terry Venables' 20-man squad, he was playing in all five games.

Southgate is a man with the right attitude. Of course he still smarts from the memories of Euro '96, but he believes life goes on, and that hard work will bring both him and England rewards to make that memory redundant.

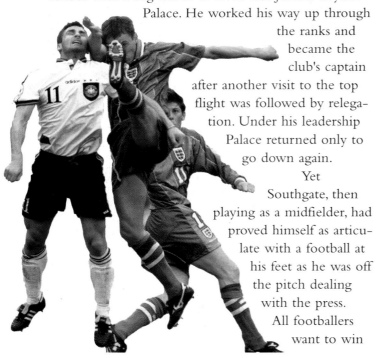

Born in Watford but brought up near Crawley in Sussex, Southgate left school with a bag full of O levels and joined Crystal Palace. He worked his way up through the ranks and became the club's captain after another visit to the top flight was followed by relegation. Under his leadership Palace returned only to go down again.

Yet Southgate, then playing as a midfielder, had proved himself as articulate with a football at his feet as he was off the pitch dealing with the press.

All footballers want to win trophies and while Southgate had played and lost in three major semi-finals with Palace, the chance to move to Aston Villa offered him a better opportunity to realize his ambitions.

Villa recognized his potential and paid £2.5 million for him in June 1995. Brian Little had clearly seen that Southgate was the sort of utility player needed to make things happen for Villa. He moved Southgate to the defence, and the rest has been plain sailing.

Southgate played in the Villa team that won the 1996 Coca-Cola Cup, beating Leeds 3-0, and became an increasingly influential member of the side. He was eventually made captain at the start of the 1997–98 season.

His strength lies in his ability to learn and to respond to situations. He is a defender who likes to bring the ball out of defence rather than hoof it upfield, and if needs be he will slot into the midfield again and play a battling game. Venables became a big fan and Glenn Hoddle, his successor, has been equally impressed.

Like Sol Campbell, Southgate looked at home in the international environment after only a few games in an England shirt. France '98 will be his chance to settle an old score. He is a man who needs no more motivation than that.

Ian Wright

Club: Arsenal
Previous clubs: Crystal Palace
Height: 5'9"
Born: 3 November 1963
International debut: v Cameroon 2-0
(Wembley) 6 February 1991

'No defender likes running towards his own goal, and if you're willing to go in there all the time, your marker will lose concentration and then it's up to you to finish.'

One of the great characters in modern football, Ian Wright was a late starter in the professional game, already in his early twenties by the time he made the Crystal Palace first team. Since then Wright has been making up for lost time.

At Palace he became a hero as he formed a devastating striking combination with Mark Bright, and the South London club enjoyed a surge to the top which saw them reach a first-ever FA Cup Final and then finish third in the old First Division.

Wright, having fought back from a broken leg, came on as a substitute in that FA Cup Final with Manchester United and scored twice before Palace lost the replay 1-0.

Signed by George Graham for Arsenal for £2.5 million in September 1991, Wright has gone on to become a Highbury legend, scoring goals as if they are going out of fashion and breaking Cliff Bastin's club record.

Controversy, however, has also stalked Wright, with his enthusiasm sometimes getting the better of him and leading to an over-the-top reaction. He has been in trouble more times than he would care to remember for clashes with match officials and opponents. For all that, however, Wright does appear contrite and he has the explosive pace and daring to light up many a cold Saturday afternoon. Give him a sniff of goal and more often than not the unexpected does happen and Wright ends up on the scoresheet.

He has found the international stage more difficult. It took him nine games to register his first goal for England – scored in a crucial World Cup qualifying match with Poland in 1993. His international career then went on hold and he was left out of the side throughout 1996.

Brought back by Glenn Hoddle, and a key player in England's Tournoi de France win in 1997, Wright scored a memorable goal against Italy and then set one up for Paul Scholes to show that, even though he is in his mid-thirties, there is still plenty of life in him. He then went on to play a superb game in Rome, where England got the draw with Italy they needed to reach France '98. Wright was denied a goal by the post. A character to lift the squad, Wright might not be a first choice when Hoddle has all his options available, but he is more than a handy substitute. He is desperate to be there.

David Seaman
A Man for All Ages

isten to a goalkeeper talk and you start to wonder how he sleeps at night. These men are born to be insomniacs, haunted by memories of the one that slipped through their fingers. The unquestionable ability of England's No. 1, David Seaman, means he will sleep better than most, but he too has his demons.

'I've always blamed myself for the Gascoigne free-kick but not for Koeman, and I don't consider Nayim was a mistake either,' said Seaman. 'It was one of those freak things. I've looked at the video hundreds of times and my positioning was right. No, my confidence wasn't shaken by that goal – but my heart was.'

Gascoigne's was in the FA Cup semi-final in 1991 in which Arsenal lost to Tottenham. Ronald Koeman's was for Holland in 1993 and ended England's attempt to qualify for the 1994 World Cup finals. Nayim's was for Real Zaragoza in the 1995 Cup Winners' Cup Final in Paris. Those goals still lurk in the man's mind. They say goalkeepers are mad – the truth is that they have memories like elephants.

This anguish seems strange from a goalkeeper who is a jovial, easy-going giant of a man. Seaman is an avid fisherman known to disappear to the waterside for days on end, but one is left wondering just what he sees when, in solitude, he gazes into deep, still waters. Here too, no doubt, he frets over the ones that get away.

It is all too easy to forget Seaman's finest moments – think how Arsenal reached that final against Real Zaragoza. In a penalty shoot-out against Sampdoria, Seaman pulled it out of the bag three times, blocking penalties from Mihajlovic and Jugovic and then reaching up to push away a blistering shot from Lombardo. When England reached the semi-finals of the European Championship in 1996, they did it by beating Spain in a penalty shoot-out. And who was it who proved to be the irresistible last line of defence? David Seaman. Earlier in the tournament he had killed off Scotland's hopes with another penalty save in normal play to deny Gary McAllister.

For all that, it is no good telling an anguished goalkeeper to forget about the odd mistake and think about the great saves because they don't seem able to do this; they will always find a flaw where there isn't one and the only time their consciences are entirely clear is when facing a penalty. And saving them is becoming an increasingly important part of the goal-keeper's art. Memories of the World Cup in America four years ago and Euro '96 point to the shoot-out again playing a large part in France '98. Luckily, Seaman is not inhibited or intimidated by the prospect. He is a man who does his homework so that, come the crunch, there is some appliance of science.

Reel back again to that game for Arsenal against Sampdoria. Seaman noted that both Mihajlovic and Jugovic attacked the ball with an arched run, suggesting that they would hook the ball. Seaman, for his part, dummied and then – expecting the hook – flung him-self in the right direction on both occasions.

After his heroics in Euro '96 he said: 'I really loved the penalty shoot-outs, because that's the only time a goalkeeper has the chance to grab the headlines. Just after the tournament finished I went to Wimbledon with Paul Ince to watch the tennis. As we walked to our seats on the Centre Court, suddenly there was this huge roar and everyone stood up. It took ages to make out that it was for us! And Pete Sampras was leading the cheering. I realized then the huge impact that Euro '96 had made on everyone.'

Born and brought up in Rotherham, Seaman was taken on as an apprentice by the club he supported – Leeds United. But it didn't work out. Rejected and hurt, he wondered what he was going to do but Peterborough came in with an offer of £4,000 and even though he didn't have the faintest idea where it was, he grabbed the opportunity with both hands.

Seaman's input into the England campaign cannot be underestimated. Arsene Wenger, his club manager, said: 'You can be the most fantastic team in the world and you will never win anything important if you do not have a top-quality goalkeeper. He can earn you as many points as a top striker. David's strengths are his intelligence and his analysis of the game and after that I would say his technique.'

All those qualities will be required in France but at least no one will spend time worrying about Seaman – he is Mr Reliable. A man with presence, he stands 6'4" and has hands like shovels. There is a quiet air of confidence about him that seeps into those around him; no bad thing given the hothouse environment of the World Cup. Nor are there many frills to Seaman, always willing with an autograph and forever chuckling. George Graham says that if you are a lousy joke-teller but want a good response, then tell it to Seaman because the laugh is guaranteed. 'Well, if someone tells a joke and it's awful,' said Seaman, 'I can't say it is terrible, I haven't got that in me. You just laugh to make them feel better.'

Then there was the time when Arsenal played Manchester United in the 1993 Charity Shield. Again it came down to penalties, only this time Seaman was the taker, not the saver. Of course he made a complete hash of it and Graham was incensed. 'It was the worst penalty I have ever seen and we lost the game because of it,' said Graham. 'When he turned to walk back up the field I was there to give him an almighty roasting but then I looked at his big face and he was laughing.'

That sort of generous spirit even extends to his rivals. In the England pecking order over recent years

he has been challenged by David James at Liverpool and Ian Walker at Tottenham. James's chances faded badly after a series of blunders towards the end of the 1996–97 season saw Liverpool slide from a challenging position in the Premiership. It left the desolate James forlornly blaming his addiction to computer games for his loss of form. Walker, too, received some flak for being beaten on his near post in England's only defeat in qualifying for France – the 1-0 loss to Italy at Wembley in February 1997. Seaman's sympathy was swift and heartfelt as he phoned both men to wish them well.

'I go out of my way to say good luck to every keeper and I always shake hands with them,' he said. 'There's a special bond between keepers that you don't tend to get with outfield players. I've had it, been through it and it's hard to take. You go home in despair sometimes and try to forget about it, distance yourself from the disappointment but it's hard. Friendship between goalkeepers doesn't go on all the time but I just felt very sorry for both David and Ian because what happened to them can happen to any goalkeeper – and will happen again.

'Mind you, I can't remember Peter Shilton ringing me up when I was having a hard time and it is when you are struggling that you find out who your friends are – but when you play for England the pressure is on.'

Painful experience has put him in a position where he can give the right answer to a goalkeeper down on his luck. 'I need to be playing all the time to maintain my consistency,' he said. 'How you handle the down-side of goalkeeping is a real test of the person you are. All you can do is make sure you train properly and work hard and slowly your confidence will come back. You can never put your finger on it but suddenly the games start going right.'

Coached by Bob Wilson at Arsenal, Seaman and the rest of the goalkeeping fraternity almost exist in their own closet world. Wilson, now a TV pundit, but once the main man at Arsenal, is in no doubt that they don't come any better than Seaman.

'He's been around long enough to not have a problem with nerves on the big occasion, but having said that, there's no danger of him being over confident,' said Wilson. 'He has made the England No. 1 jersey his own and if he continues to play as he has done all season England will be fine.

'I work with him at close quarters all week and I believe David is as good as Pat Jennings at his peak. Pat was the best I ever saw. David just fills the goal – fills it with calm presence.

'People think he is a laid-back Yorkshireman but he's a real student of goalkeeping and there's nothing I can teach him. I just keep him ticking over because he's so hyper-critical of his every performance that he never stops thinking of ways to improve his game – he takes every goal as a personal insult and has an intense desire and determination to stay at the top of his profession.'

Wilson, in pinpointing Seaman's determination, also hits on another strength – a desire to learn all the time. 'Bob wouldn't tell me if he thought that in his day he was a better goalkeeper than me, because his best asset is that he builds your confidence,' said Seaman. 'If you have a bad day training he can build your morale and he's also tactically aware of what goalkeepers need to work on, too.'

There is no room for a bad day at the office during a World Cup and, to return to the point about Seaman's quiet influence on the team, it is perhaps significant that of the eight qualifying games played, the one defeat came when Walker was in goal and then another defeat, in a friendly against Chile, happened with Nigel Martyn as

the No. 1. Martyn, however, could not be faulted for either of the goals conceded.

So what happens in the changing room in the tense half-hour before kick-off? At Wembley, Peter Shilton had a board fixed to the wall in the shower room. He would disappear there and bounce the ball off it, sharpening himself for the action to come. Seaman's preparations are different but predictable. 'I don't psyche myself up or sit in the corner and concentrate extra hard. I'm quiet and I know what I have to do.'

For a man who left school before taking any exams, Seaman has not done badly. As a goalkeeper he doesn't need to prove himself to anyone but himself, and that is what keeps him going. His real talent, however, is his gentle off-pitch manner – anyone who can draw the sting of a raging George Graham with a laugh must be pretty special.

All players dream of the World Cup and England's hopes look bright for France. This is the ultimate challenge, the chance to be the biggest fish in the world pond. Much, however, will depend on how well Seaman sleeps, aided not by a cup of Horlicks but that best sedative of all, clean sheets.

David Beckham
Cockney Lad to Megastar

It took just 27 seconds for Bryan Robson to make his mark on seven-year-old David Beckham back in 1982. Now, 16 years on, it's Beckham's turn to turn the heads of the Teletubby generation.

As a football-mad youngster, Beckham was brought up on the best of England – Robson's quick-fire goal against France in Spain in 1982 is his earliest World Cup memory, and video tape has embellished the word of legend with vivid proof. Goals from the likes of Bobby Charlton and Glenn Hoddle were – and still are – an inspiration to him.

'My dad told me all about Bobby Charlton and showed me some of his goals on video, they were unbelievable,' says Beckham who, as an 11-year-old, went on to meet the Manchester United and England legend at soccer skills school. The advice then, as it is now, is: 'When you see the goal – shoot.'

And still Beckham listens. Still he is engagingly in awe of Charlton, who he sees regularly at Manchester United. 'He helps me a lot and was brilliant on the course when there must have been 1,000 other kids. I wasn't the only one to get good advice,' Beckham remembers.

Ability and God-given talent are one thing; the capacity to look, listen and learn, another. Beckham has both, plus a level-headed attitude that would make him a role model even if he wasn't such a good footballer. And all this achieved while on a head-turning rocket rise from being just one of a number of lucky young footballers to an out-and-out superstar.

'You can always pick up tips from other players. I learned a lot from Eric Cantona at United and playing in the Champions' League helps – then it is practice and technique. Watch Brazil and you will see a centre-half pick up the ball, run with it then shoot from 25 yards – it all looks so natural, so comfortable,' he says. 'Sadly in this country the reaction is cynical, we build good players up as great players and then delight in knocking them down. Score a great goal and it is a fluke – yet if an Italian or Brazilian did the same thing, you'd expect it.'

Beckham's playing response to that is to score

great and improbable goals himself and with such regularity that, when the public see or read about another superlative Beckham strike, they take it for what it is – entirely natural.

England and France '98 looms large in the mind and despite all that he has achieved, Beckham is still learning all the time.

'Playing for England is like being with a good club – and not just because there are a number of my United team-mates in the side, there is a great atmosphere and a common purpose,' he says. 'We bond well, laugh together and argue – but not in a damaging way. It is a learning curve, a privilege to be there with players like Paul Ince, Ian Wright and Alan Shearer. Shearer really is the model player, fantastic on the pitch and brilliant off it, a really nice bloke. By being in the company of these guys I can become a better player.'

A heavy domestic and European season that culminates in a metronomic swing of fixtures Wednesday and Saturday, Wednesday and Saturday, will have taken its toll on some, but for Beckham that is part and parcel of being a professional footballer. As he says, it is better to be playing than not.

The beautiful game is still a source of much pleasure for him, and while he admits that his rise could lead to some damaging distractions, he has surrounded himself with people – including his parents and sisters back in Essex – who are aware of the pitfalls.

'I've not had to make a conscious effort to keep a level head because I'm fairly quiet and I'm lucky to have people around me who will help, who know I need to get away sometimes and are aware there has to be a release,' he says.

Even so, if Beckham was walking along a secluded getaway Caribbean island and came across a group of youngsters having a kick-around, would he join in? 'You bet,' he says. 'Nothing would stop me.'

Beckham might be a star made inaccessible by the unforgiving spotlight of fame that blinds most of his waking hours, but a prima donna? Never.

Sol Campbell
FA School of Excellence

Pass and move forward are as much words of wisdom from a coaching manual as they are an accurate description of Sol Campbell's career path. His is a story of increasingly testing challenges taken and passed with first class honours.

The 23-year-old Tottenham defender started with Sunday side Rippleway near Newham in Essex where he was born. He failed to be selected by Essex Schools, but was picked up by Tottenham, sailed through the FA School of Excellence at Lilleshall and then returned to White Hart Lane to rise through the ranks; youth team, reserves, firsts and then England. By the end of the World Cup, Campbell could well be an automatic pick for the tournament all-star side. Throw down the gauntlet to this man and he will pick it up. He not only likes a challenge – he needs one to stay on top of his game.

'Every level I've reached has seen the skill factor rise and in international football you are up against players at the very top of their profession,' he said. 'You have to dig deeper, discover more about yourself and get on with the job and improve, not just to keep up with your opponents, but to keep ahead of those other players after your place.

'That's what keeps you going through a long season, always having something to aim for. You have to be on the ball and give as good as you take. There are players that have given me a hard time but then that's because they've been on top of their game and I've been off mine – another time and it will be different.'

Playing for England means a different approach to matches than at Tottenham, where the heavy schedule gives little time for reflection. For almost a week before an international, the players are brought together.

'It is a case of making a slow start, you all get used to each other for a few days and then it starts to gel so that by the time of the match we are absolutely united. International football keeps you sharp, you must hold your concentration and while the build-up from the back is slower than in the Premiership, once a team is going forward the pace picks up,' he says.

'You can watch videos and learn about the opposition, know which way certain strikers like to turn. Concentration has to be absolute and you have to react fast.

'There is an edge to international football that you don't get at club level because it is not so easy to go out and put a bad result behind you.

'Our draw for the World Cup is a good one but at that level you must respect all your opponents because they have earned the right to be there and no match is going to be easy. It is a case of being fresh and sharp and going out to play your own game.

'Afterwards you can talk about a good match, but I don't believe in doing that until a side has been beaten.'

Campbell – 6'2" and famed for his huge appetite – has become an automatic choice for England, with his calm and solid defending since his debut against Hungary in 1996. His emergence is part of a new, young England, that has developed and matured impressively under Glenn Hoddle. He likes to relax; in fact he is determined to get the right balance between rest and training as a long season becomes a marathon.

'It's about discipline, both with the work you do on the game and how you look after yourself. You get to know what you need from yourself to be at your best. Playing for England is the highest honour and if reaching the World Cup Final means only a two-week break in the summer of 1998 – then I won't be complaining!'

The Road to Glory

The World Cup is the ultimate prize. A glowing golden trophy that sits tantalizingly before the world's football nations but once every four years. It has been won by only six nations in 58 years – and the number wanting to win it is growing all the time.

England are one of those exclusive six – memories of 1966 are still fresh in the mind, kept alive by legend, fact and modern culture. Even those who weren't born then know all about it.

'They think it's all over, it is now,' said Kenneth Wolstenholme as Geoff Hurst burst forward to score his third and England's fourth at Wembley on that Saturday – 30 July 1966. Today, Wolstenholme's observation is used as the title for a sporting comedy show and

England no longer just dream of repeating that glorious moment – they truly believe they can do it again and become World Champions. There have been more than 30 years of hurting since 1966 and that 4-2 win over West Germany; false dawns and promises that have turned to dust.

England did well in 1970 in defence of their title. There was an epic match with Brazil and no disgrace in losing 1-0. They still reached the quarter-finals where they faced the foe of 1966 again, West Germany. England went 2-0 up but suddenly the Germans hit back, scored twice to equalize and won the match in extra-time. In the space of those 120 minutes in Mexico, England went from defending champions to former champions and took a trip into a footballing wilderness.

England did not reach the finals in West Germany in 1974. Alf Ramsey, later to be knighted, stepped down and first Joe Mercer, as caretaker manager, and then Don Revie took charge. Ron Greenwood took over from 1977 until 1982, but there was more disappointment when the Argentina World Cup came and went without England's presence.

At least England were at the party in Spain in 1982 and they romped through the first round with three wins out of three. Bryan Robson took just 27 seconds to put England ahead against France in their first match of the tournament. The second stage that year was another group contest, each group made up of three teams. But England did not score enough goals to carry them through and departed with a record of three won, two drawn and none lost.

A real revival was evident during Bobby Robson's reign when England reached the Mexico finals of 1986. From the group matches they went on to the quarter-finals, where Maradona's infamous 'Hand of God' goal ended England's interest.

Robson was at the helm when England played in Italy in 1990 and he came within a penalty kick of joining Alf Ramsey as a legend of England footballing success. They reached the knockout stages, beating Belgium in the last 16 when David Platt swivelled and scored with virtually the last kick of extra-time. That was 1-0 to England.

Next up were Cameroon, the pride of Africa, powered by innocent skills and the unforgettable enthusiasm of Roger Milla, a player in his late thirties. England won, after a struggle, thanks to two Gary Lineker penalties, 3-2.

And there they were again – the old foe Germany. A pulsating and intriguing semi-final ended 1-1 and went to penalties. England bit the dust as Chris Waddle and Stuart Pearce were foiled. It was an agonizing way to depart. England really believed that they could have won that year, and on the evidence of the Final – West Germany beat Argentina 1-0 – there was little reason to question the validity of such speculation.

Graham Taylor was the next manager to try – and fail – to get England back to the heights they had achieved in the past. England did not make it to the World Cup in the USA in 1994, but the seeds of a real revival were about to be sown.

Taylor, pressurized throughout, lampooned and ridiculed in the English press, resigned and Terry Venables was put in charge. The former Crystal Palace, Queens Park Rangers, Tottenham and Barcelona manager was much admired in the game by his peers, who recognized in him a sharp tactical brain and a strong motivator. Venables was the sort of coach to shape England's cloth to the ability of its players.

His target was the 1996 European Championship, being hosted on home soil. England had to do well. There were home expectations to be fulfilled; there was home pride that England players – joined by more and more foreigners in the Premiership – could hold up their end; and most of all, there was the incentive of a major prize.

Venables' magic worked. He created a side that could do what he wanted and England opened the tournament on familiar territory at Wembley with a nervous 1-1 draw against Switzerland. A week later they settled some old scores when they beat Scotland 2-0 at the same venue. It was a victory fashioned by Paul Gascoigne – ironically an Englishman plying his club football trade in Scotland with Rangers.

Four days later England produced one of their finest performances in living memory when they played Holland at Wembley on a warm summer evening. England were irresistible as Holland were cut to ribbons by such an incisive passing game that only those who witnessed it would have believed it possible.

Shearer scored from the penalty spot and it was 1-0 to the hosts at half-time. Next Teddy Sheringham scored, Shearer added the third and, with just over an hour gone, Sheringham tucked away the fourth. There was a consolation goal for the Dutch, but the undeniable truth was that they had been hammered – and the result sent shock waves around Europe.

In the quarter-final England needed penalties to beat Spain after a 0-0 draw, and then it was on to the semi-final: Germany again. England went ahead after three minutes thanks to Shearer, only for Germany to equalize. It was 1-1 at full-time and although England pressed – and went desperately close to scoring in extra-time – it came down to penalties.

It was neck-and-neck until the sixth penalty for England. Up stepped Gareth Southgate of Aston Villa, a relative newcomer to the England ranks. He struck the ball too softly, his shot was saved and the clinical

Germans were a kick away from the Final. It was an opportunity they were not going to miss. In fact they went on to win the tournament.

Venables had announced he was going, whatever the result of Euro '96, and it was left to Glenn Hoddle to mop up after the disappointment. The changeover, handled with good sense and an eye on the future, happened smoothly enough as the former Tottenham and England player, and more recently Chelsea manager, picked up where Venables had left off. He inherited a squad that was starting to believe it could win international tournaments; a group of players who, after Euro '96, had no reason to question their abilities in comparison with the rest of the world. Better than that, he had his own ideas; a vision for England that he knew was within reach.

Respected by his peers and trusted by his players, Hoddle's job was to take England to the 1998 World Cup. There were a few friendlies along the way, but mostly it was the real thing and World Cup qualification. Tough away wins in Poland, Georgia and Moldova were achieved with style and a surprising sense of calm. Hoddle's team cooled the raging Italian passions in Rome and won through to the finals on merit: 15 goals scored, two conceded and just one defeat in eight matches.

In between times there was the Tournoi de France, where England beat Italy 2-0, France 1-0 and lost to Brazil 1-0. It was good enough to win them the competition and to prove that England can keep company with the very best in world football.

France is just a short hop away and England can see that famous World Cup trophy tantalizingly within reach. Minds are very much concentrated on it. England can boast it gave the world football, and now it would like to reclaim the ultimate prize – the World Cup.

The Green Flag Years

Sport, as with everyday life, is about knowing what you want and then giving it your best to achieve that aim.

For England back in early 1995 the road ahead was clear. There were new sponsors in the form of Green Flag, a new coach in Terry Venables and Euro '96 was a definite destination. Beyond that, to be pondered on and achieved, was the World Cup. Exactly how England were to get there was in the lap of the gods and the luck of the draw. Running the team, picking the players and deciding the tactics, however, was something that could be controlled.

Failure to reach USA '94 had led to the usual fall-out – new brooms, new coaches and Graham Taylor resigning. The pain for everyone involved in that attempt was acute, memories of Taylor's torment in Holland in 1993 made all the more intense by a fly-on-the-wall TV documentary that did not relent as the pain of defeat, the slings and arrows of outrageous fortune, left visible scars on the man before our very eyes as Holland beat England in a crucial qualifying match.

Taylor's plight was made worse by the relative success of the previous campaign in Italy 1990, where England reached the semi-finals and would have probably won the World Cup but for a penalty shoot-out loss to Germany.

The past, though, is gone. A new dawn beckoned, an age where things could be done differently.

And so Terry Venables, appointed on 28 January 1994, started the new era with a 1-0 win at Wembley over European Champions Denmark. It got better as morale was repaired with a 5-0 win over Greece, before a 0-0 draw with Norway. The USA were beaten 2-0, there was a draw with Romania 1-1, then a victory, 1-0, over Nigeria. It was a spectacular beginning for Venables, a man who had said that if he had still been managing Tottenham Hotspur, he would not have taken the job.

England were on the way back and more support for the cause came with the backing of Green Flag, who hosted their first international at Wembley with a friendly – but against Uruguay, twice winners of the world's greatest sporting contest.

29 March 1995
ENGLAND 0 URUGUAY 0

DAVID PLATT was the England captain as the unbeaten run to Venables' campaign continued – but it was hardly the feast of football that the billing suggested. England showed sterling defensive qualities with Tony Adams, of Arsenal, and Gary Pallister, of Manchester United, holding firm.

Then in the second half the National School of Excellence – the England football academy at Lilleshall – celebrated its first graduate to full international honours when Nick Barmby, then of Tottenham, came on for Peter Beardsley. He was followed six minutes later by another Lilleshall student – Andy Cole.

The domestic season then took centre stage with Everton surprisingly beating Manchester United to take the FA Cup while in the Premiership Blackburn were crowned champions. Those matters resolved, Venables could concentrate on England with time to work with his squad as they prepared for the Umbro Cup. The mini-tournament had a mixed guest list – Japan, Sweden and world champions Brazil.

3 June 1995
ENGLAND 2 JAPAN 1

THE UNBEATEN RECORD was kept intact, and never really threatened, but the win was hard-earned

when with three minutes remaining David Platt saved the day, scoring from the penalty spot.

England had taken the lead thanks to Darren Anderton's goal three minutes into the second half. It came after he played a neat one-two with Alan Shearer. The Japanese, full of invention and running, refused to give up and surprisingly equalized when Masami Ihara headed home.

England pressed hard as the clock ran down and luck seemed to be out, until John Scales' shot was handled on the line. Perhaps not the most convincing of wins, but there were fair excuses. The domestic season had left Venables with an injury list which prevented him from fielding his first-choice side.

8 June 1995
ENGLAND 3 SWEDEN 3

THE BATTLING QUALITIES were to the fore as England faced defeat for the first time under Venables. Sweden led 3-1 with two minutes remaining and for a side without the heart of this England it would have been game, set and match.

Teddy Sheringham had scored England's opening goal at Elland Road but incessant raids in an action-packed match yielded no tangible rewards – all efforts halted by luck and great goalkeeping from Ravelli, winning his 126th cap. Then the breakthrough: Paul Gascoigne, on as a super-sub, floated a free-kick to the far post where David Platt headed it home.

The match restarted, England swept back on the attack Anderton drove in the equalizer from outside the box. The result left England needing to beat Brazil in their final match to win the tournament.

11 June 1995
ENGLAND 1 BRAZIL 3

IT HAD TO COME – defeat. But at least Venables' team went down in style and hinted at a shape and form that could develop for the better. More importantly, Brazil were the sort of opponents England needed for properly gauging their progress.

Wembley was buzzing from the start and the players were caught up in the positive atmosphere, but just as Brazil seemed to have weathered the storm, England scored. Graeme Le Saux struck a tremendous volley from outside the penalty area. In the second half, however, Brazil showed just why they are World Champions and incisive finishing left England with a 3-1 defeat. It was time for a break, to prepare for a new season and to mull over what had happened.

6 September 1995
ENGLAND 0 COLOMBIA 0

EURO '96 WAS NOW the main focus and Colombia, late replacements for Croatia, provided an entertaining challenge on a night that had one outstanding moment.

Jamie Redknapp floated the ball towards the centre of the Colombian goal where Rene Higuita, the goalkeeper, ducked beneath it, did a flip in the air and backheeled it away. The scorpion had struck.

Seven of the England team had ten or less caps, but even so it was a solid and entertaining performance which would have brought more tangible rewards but for the woodwork saving the Colombians on three occasions. Gascoigne certainly enjoyed himself on an evening made for footballing showmen – the Colombians had Freddy Rincon and Carlos Valderrama in their side.

11 October 1995
NORWAY 0 ENGLAND 0

THE FIRST AWAY MATCH in six goes – and a dull draw. Norway were defending a four-year unbeaten home record and that seemed to be the priority. In the early exchanges the home side tried the long ball tactic but found the England defence well able to cope.

There were two scares for England, the second late in the match when an unsighted David Seaman had to react late to push a shot round the post. In attack England were fairly blunt, although Steve McManaman increasingly threatened.

15 November 1995
ENGLAND 3 SWITZERLAND 1

ENGLAND CONCEDED A GOAL at one of the worst possible moments – four minutes before half-time. Yet they came out flying in the second half and, needing a quick reply, managed it.

Stuart Pearce hammered in a shot following a quick corner routine featuring Paul Gascoigne and Steve McManaman. A glancing header from Teddy Sheringham put England ahead then Steve Stone – capped for the first time as a substitute in Norway – poked home the ball after an Alan Shearer shot had been spilled by the Swiss goalkeeper.

12 December 1995
ENGLAND 1 PORTUGAL 1

PORTUGAL WERE ONE of the bookies' pre-tournament favourites for Euro '96. A side that had grown up together through Under-19 football, and one that had an understanding forged by experience, provided a worthy challenge. England played a diamond-formation with Paul Gascoigne the anchorman, but it was the man of the moment, Steve Stone, who put England ahead with a crashing Bobby Charlton-like shot. Paulo Alves then slid home an equalizer in the 59th minute. England might still have won it: new cap Gareth Southgate hit the bar with a header with almost his very first touch in international football.

27 March 1996
ENGLAND 1 BULGARIA 0

ENGLAND RULED THE ROOST in a match which saw the Bulgarians – World Cup semi-finalists in 1994 – showing little imagination: they left Hristo Stoitchkov, their star striker, out of the side.

Les Ferdinand, using all his strength and speed, put England ahead after Teddy Sheringham had played him in, and there could have been more goals for England as the home side, welcoming Paul Ince back, dominated the first half. Bulgaria were more daring in the second half but England coped with ease.

24 April 1996
ENGLAND 0 CROATIA 0

A SOLID PERFORMANCE which saw England hold one of Europe's more fancied sides in a game that, in its early stages, had more than a touch of the strategic chess gambit to it. Croatia strung intricate passes across Wembley; a spider's web of movement.

England watched and were patient and there were chances for both sides. As the match ebbed, so Croatia started to wilt and Steve McManaman hit the post with ten minutes remaining. Teddy Sheringham failed to tuck away the rebound.

18 May 1996
ENGLAND 3 HUNGARY 0

IT WAS GOODBYE TO WEMBLEY until Euro '96, and England left on a high. Darren Anderton headed home Teddy Sheringham's cross after Les Ferdinand had missed it. England went in at half-time 1-0 up and David Seaman had not had to deal with a single shot.

In the second half David Platt scored after Paul Ince's free-kick caught the Hungary defence napping. The final touch came from Anderton with his second goal of the match. Venables then gave two Tottenham players their first caps – Ian Walker took over from Seaman and Sol Campbell came on for Ince. It was an easy win.

23 May 1996
CHINA 0 ENGLAND 3

A MISSIONARY TRIP TO BEIJING to play China in the Workers' Stadium before a crowd of 65,000 could so easily have gone wrong. Instead England were the very model of diplomatic authority.

Tony Adams was back in defence for his first match in four months and was clearly in charge. Paul Gascoigne buzzed and Nick Barmby scored twice. The first time he hit the post, gathered the rebound and completed the job himself. The next came in the second half when Gascoigne played him in. Gascoigne then added a third. Robbie Fowler replaced Alan Shearer late on and posed a considerable threat.

EURO '96

Terry Venables was going for all or nothing. He was not going to stay on as England coach after Euro '96 so this was to be his one and only major tournament – and the nation expected much.

How would those friendlies have prepared England for a proper test? The trouble with not having to qualify is that the team is not match-sharp on the international stage – a problem to be faced in the World Cup by France the hosts, and the reigning champions, Brazil.

And whatever anyone says, playing even top-notch friendlies is no substitute for the cut and thrust of football where the result means everything – economies have gone up and down on the feel-good factor of the right football result at the right time.

8 June 1996
ENGLAND 1 SWITZERLAND 1

THE DROUGHT WAS OVER for Alan Shearer. The match was 23 minutes old when Paul Ince threaded the ball through, Shearer with an elusive run had beaten the offside trap and was in on goal. His shot beat the goalkeeper at the near post. England had played 14 matches since Shearer had last scored.

That should have settled England, but Switzerland were determined challengers and the host nation were increasingly living on their nerves.

Then, eight minutes from the end, the ball hit Stuart Pearce on the hand and the referee gave a penalty, considered by many to be rather harsh. Turkyilmaz equalized and that was it.

15 June 1996
ENGLAND 2 SCOTLAND 0

IT WAS SEVEN YEARS since they had last met, 11 since Scotland had beaten England – yet at Wembley on a summer afternoon it was the visitors who showed more grit in the first half. England coped well enough, then in the second half raised the stakes. Shearer, now that he had ended his international goal drought, was looking very sharp, and scored after Steve McManaman played in Gary Neville. His cross beat the cover and Andy Goram in the Scotland goal – and there was Shearer.

Gordon Durie then fell over Tony Adams' leg in a tackle and Scotland were awarded a penalty. David Seaman, however, anticipated right and forced McAllister's shot over the bar. Scotland were made to suffer as England came forward to make the match safe and did so when Paul Gascoigne scored a peach. There was no way back for the visitors.

Golden Goal

PAUL GASCOIGNE has built a reputation out of making the improbable happen and his goal for England against Scotland in Euro '96 was a classic – inventive, daring and skilful.

Gascoigne ran forward, picked up the ball, flicked it over Colin Hendry and darted past him to bury the shot way beyond Andy Goram's reach.

Wembley erupted, not just because it was one over the auld enemy, but because they had witnessed a truly great piece of skill and a very special goal.

18 June 1996
ENGLAND 4 HOLLAND 1

ENGLAND WERE ELECTRIC and this single result spelled it out to the world – they were back in business.

Teddy Sheringham released Steve McManaman in the 23rd minute and he charged down the inside right channel. Ince made a run into the box, and when the cross came, he flicked the ball on and was sent flying. Penalty England and Alan Shearer obliged.

In the second half Sheringham powered home a header from Paul Gascoigne's corner and the two of them then combined to set up Shearer who crashed home England's third. Sheringham then made it four, reacting quickest when Edwin van der Sar in the Holland goal could only parry Anderton's drive.

A Dutch consolation goal late on was enough to keep them in the competition – on goal difference from Scotland.

22 June 1996
ENGLAND 0 SPAIN 0

AGAINST AN ORGANIZED and, for that matter, skilful side, England had a real challenge on their hands in the quarter-final against Spain at Wembley.

It took solid performances from Tony Adams and Gareth Southgate to keep them out – and a touch of luck. Spain had the ball in the net after 33 minutes, but England were reprieved thanks to an offside call.

A couple of times Spanish players fell in the England penalty area, but the referee was not interested.

Then in the second half England came into it more, both Alan Shearer and Teddy Sheringham missed good chances and after half an hour of extra-time it was down to penalties.

Spain missed one and had one saved. England were spot on – including Stuart Pearce who was exorcizing the ghost of the missed penalty in Italy that had cost England a World Cup Final place in 1990.

26 June 1996
ENGLAND 1 GERMANY 1

THREE MINUTES GONE and England were ahead. Gascoigne's corner was touched on by Tony Adams and there was Alan Shearer to score. Wembley erupted and so did millions of sitting rooms up and down the country.

This was a clash that brought memories of great games between the two countries flooding back. England 4 West Germany 2 in 1966; England 2 West Germany 3 in 1970; England 1 West Germany 1 (Germany won on penalties) in 1990. England, it was felt, were due a bit of luck. Less than 15 minutes had gone and Germany were level through Stefan Kuntz.

It was nip and tuck, heart-stopping stuff in extra-time and if either side scored, the match would be over. Darren Anderton hit the post, Paul Gascoigne

was the width of a cigarette paper from connecting with Alan Shearer's cross, the Germans had a header disallowed. It was down to penalties and a moment of misery for Gareth Southgate, whose shot was saved. England were out of the competition.

AFTER EURO '96

Terry Venables packed his bags and cleared his desk, but had time to leave a goodwill message for the new man, Glenn Hoddle. For Venables the World Cup was to beckon through a surprise route when he was offered, and accepted, the post of coach to Australia. For Hoddle, the World Cup prospects with England were brighter and more realistic than those for Venables.

Yet the old England boss gave it his best shot. He sparked something of a revolution down under by taking Australia to a play-off with Iran for a winner-take-all prize, a trip to France. The first match ended 1-1 and on home soil the Australians were 2-0 up when disaster struck. Two sloppy goals and it was 2-2 – Iran went through on the away goal and Venables had failed. By that stage, however, Hoddle knew he was going to France for the World Cup finals.

1 September 1996
WORLD CUP QUALIFIER
MOLDOVA 0 ENGLAND 3 (see page 53)

9 October 1996
WORLD CUP QUALIFIER
ENGLAND 2 POLAND 1 (see page 54)

Golden Goal

A TIGHTER MATCH THAN EXPECTED was settled by a classic Alan Shearer goal. With the score standing at 1-1, Shearer picked up the ball just on the edge of the penalty area. Ahead of him was Les

Ferdinand with two markers breathing down his neck. Shearer shot, the ball hit Ferdinand and bounced back to Shearer who reacted in a flash and crashed the ball into the top left-hand corner of the net. It was a great instinctive strike and invaluable to England at that stage in the match.

SHEARER'S SECOND GOAL

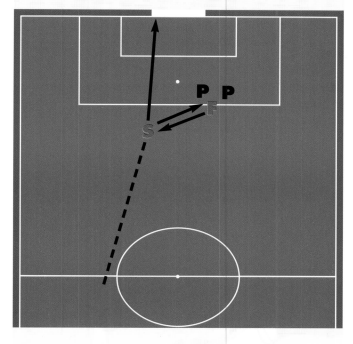

S = *Alan Shearer* **F** = *Les Ferdinand* **P** = *Polish defender*
━━ = *path of ball* **━━━━** = *path of run*

Shearer shoots straight at Ferdinand. The ball bounces back to Shearer who fires into the left-hand corner of the goal.

9 November 1996
WORLD CUP QUALIFIER

GEORGIA 0 ENGLAND 2 (see page 55)

12 February 1997
WORLD CUP QUALIFIER

ENGLAND 0 ITALY 1 (see page 56)

29 March 1997
ENGLAND 2 MEXICO 0

RELIEF FOR HODDLE in his first friendly. It was his fifth match in charge, but as his predecessors had discovered, an international match slotted into the Premiership schedule often leads to a shortage of first-choice players.

There was no Alan Shearer, whose place was taken by Robbie Fowler, and Martin Keown was in the middle of defence, while Robert Lee was drafted into the midfield. Given the changes it was no surprise that England took time to settle, but there is nothing like a goal to ease the nerves.

It came after 18 minutes. Lee released Sheringham who made his way into the box. He was stopped but the ball rebounded to Ince. His progress was halted by what was deemed an illegal challenge and Sheringham scored from the penalty spot.

In the second half, Jamie Redknapp came on for David Batty and Ian Wright for Sheringham. Wright had a header from a Graeme Le Saux cross parried, but Fowler was on hand to head home the loose ball.

30 April 1997
WORLD CUP QUALIFIER

ENGLAND 2 GEORGIA 0 (see page 57)

24 May 1997
ENGLAND 2 SOUTH AFRICA 1

ENGLAND BLOODED some new faces for this match at Old Trafford and there were eight changes from the side which, four weeks earlier, had played Georgia. Despite the score England ran the show, and Sheringham went close twice before Robert Lee put England ahead, after Philip Neville had chested the ball down.

Against the run of play, South Africa drew level, but England were soon back in their stride. Paul Gascoigne curled a free-kick against the post and then, with 15 minutes remaining, Paul Scholes played the ball on for Ian Wright who swivelled and scored.

31 May 1997
WORLD CUP QUALIFIER

POLAND 0 ENGLAND 2 (see page 58)

Golden Goal

THE CLASSIC counter-attacking goal within five minutes. England's defence was magnificent and the ball went to Paul Ince, who made great strides forward. Alan Shearer, lurking on the halfway line, made his run, collected Ince's pass and despite the close attentions of the Poland defence, carved out space and fired into the bottom left-hand corner.

SHEARER'S GOAL

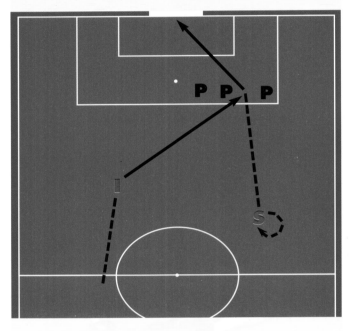

S = *Alan Shearer* **I** = *Paul Ince* **P** = *Polish defender*
■■ = *path of ball* ■■■■ = *path of run*

From a Polish attack, Paul Ince won the ball in midfield and ran forward over the halfway line. He released Shearer with a neat pass and he smashed the ball into the left-hand corner of the goal.

4 June 1997
TOURNOI DE FRANCE

ITALY 0 ENGLAND 2

A SUPERB WIN BY AN ENGLAND team driven by David Beckham and Paul Scholes against the same Italy – bar Paolo Maldini – that had beaten England at Wembley in February.

England were inventive and fast and Ian Wright, playing probably his best game for England, scored after 25 minutes.

Still England pushed on and two minutes before half-time it was 2-0. Scholes and Wright combined to carve open the Italian defence and Scholes finished the job in style.

Italy had their moments, but a well-marshalled England defence coped easily and it was England who always looked more likely to score again. 'See you in Rome,' said Cesare Maldini, the Italian coach, at the end. It was England's first win over Italy in 20 years.

Golden Goal

PAUL SCHOLES looked a natural for England when they beat Italy 2-0 in France in June 1997. He formed a potent partnership with Ian Wright and it was Scholes who set up the first goal.

Then came Scholes' moment, his first goal for England and one that announced emphatically his arrival on the international stage. Again it was the combination with Wright which provided the opening, but it was the way Scholes buried the half-chance, past the keeper from ten yards out which caught the eye.

7 June 1997
TOURNOI DE FRANCE

FRANCE 0 ENGLAND 1

A RECORD WIN IN MANY WAYS – England's sixth successive victory, the first in France since 1949 and the first defeat the hosts had suffered on home soil in three years.

England were not quite as fluent as they had been when beating Italy, but they had an eye for the main chance. There were five minutes remaining when a Teddy Sheringham cross was spilled by the French goalkeeper and Alan Shearer was on hand to clean up.

There had been chances throughout and David Seaman pulled off a sensational save to palm away a well-struck, goal-bound shot from the French midfielder Pierre Laigle. In the end England were well worth the victory and, irrespective of their result against Brazil, were winners of the tournament.

10 June 1997
TOURNOI DE FRANCE

BRAZIL 1 ENGLAND 0

ENGLAND DEFENDED well and Paul Gascoigne enjoyed the challenge of putting on a show against class opponents – but it was the Brazilians who set the pace.

Parc des Princes was filled with a samba beat and David Seaman was called upon to watch every shot, every free-kick. The best chances fell to Brazil but it was 0-0 at half-time.

England managed one quality shot, a rasping drive from Paul Ince, but came more into the match in the second half. The deadlock, however, was broken by Romário who latched on to Leonardo's pass, advanced on Seaman and poked the ball home.

England were to go close again but could not make the breakthrough, and an unbeaten away run, stretching back almost four years, was ended.

10 September 1997
WORLD CUP QUALIFIER

ENGLAND 4 MOLDOVA 0 (see page 59)

Golden Goal

SCHOLES' GOAL

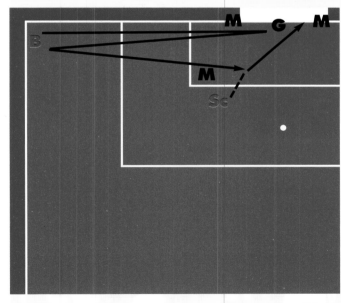

B = *David Beckham* **Sc** = *Paul Scholes*
M = *Moldova defenders* **G** = *Moldova goalkeeper*
▬ = *path of ball* ▪▪▪▪ = *path of run*

David Beckham's inswinging corner was punched back to him by the Moldova goalkeeper. Beckham looped in another cross, Scholes' marker slipped giving him room, and he dived full length to head into the top right-hand corner of the goal.

IT WAS THE MANCHESTER United connection which launched England on the road to a 4-0 win over Moldova and a place in France '98. The first goal at Wembley came from a David Beckham inswinging

corner which was punched straight back to him. He steadied and crossed again and Scholes dived full length to head home. It was a brave and crucial goal.

11 October 1997
WORLD CUP QUALIFIER

ITALY 0 ENGLAND 0 (see page 60)

15 November 1997

ENGLAND 2 CAMEROON 0

PLENTY TO CELEBRATE for England and they did so with a friendly against a team they will join in France '98. On the same night around the world lucky losers were playing it out for the few remaining places in that World Cup.

An injury to Gareth Southgate allowed England to cap West Ham's youngster Rio Ferdinand after 40 minutes and he was very solid on his debut.

Elsewhere, the likes of Andy Hinchcliffe and Robbie Fowler were assured and Sol Campbell and Paul Scholes looked more and more comfortable in England shirts.

Cameroon offered little in attack but goals still had to be scored to beat them. The first came a minute before half-time. Paul Gascoigne made the run, slipped the ball to Scholes and despite the heavy attentions of two defenders, he was still standing and able to fire home.

It was 2-0 moments later. David Beckham was released on the right, crossed, Paul Ince ducked it and Robbie Fowler was on hand to head home. England had cantered it.

From Venables to Hoddle

It is the poisoned chalice and the jewel in the crown; the job of your dreams and the job you wouldn't wish on your worst enemy. It is a situation never advertised as vacant at a Job Centre near you, but the post, call it what you will, is England manager, England coach.

Throughout the land there are hundreds of thousands of England managers sitting in front rooms and pub snugs, certain that they know how to do the job; who should be in, who should be out. In reality there have been only eight out-and-out managers and one caretaker.

Glenn Hoddle is the man of the moment, succeeding Terry Venables. The link between the two is Jimmy Armfield, the former Blackpool and England player. Armfield was recruited by the Football Association to head-hunt a manager after England failed to reach the 1994 World Cup in the USA.

Graham Taylor decided enough was enough and quit – the reality of the England post being that if you don't take the side to the World Cup then the contract will certainly run out; you either resign or suffer the humiliation of being fired. That left England in limbo. Everyone mentioned as a possible candidate for the post wanted nothing to do with it. This wasn't a hot potato – it was a radioactive hot potato.

'I don't want the job and I don't envy who gets it,' said Steve Coppell, the Crystal Palace manager and former England and Manchester United player, who was considered one of the leading contenders. 'You have got to be joking,' said Roy Hodgson, at the time the Switzerland manager, 'even the Pope would have second thoughts about taking the job.' Don Howe, Kevin Keegan and John Lyall were all mentioned and all beat a hasty retreat. Yet England could not be left with Hobson's choice and turned to Armfield to solve the problem. Armfield had a spell as manager at Leeds and while there tried to hire Venables, who he recognized as an outstanding coach.

The trouble this time was that Venables was in the middle of an acrimonious feud with Alan Sugar at Tottenham, and there were unresolved questions about his business methods. Even so Armfield, with a field full of non-runners, had to come up with someone and just any old name would not do – Venables was his man.

The appointment was made on 28 January 1994 and Venables had the luxury of knowing that for the next big date on the international footballing calendar, the European Championship, his side would be at the party. In fact, England were hosting the event.

Venables had started out at Chelsea where he made his debut in 1959, went on to Tottenham, from there to Queens Park Rangers and Crystal Palace, first as a player then as a coach. At Palace, with his mentor Malcolm Allison in charge, Venables was able to hone his skills and he led the club to the First Division. He developed the famed 'team of the eighties' – the side that was going to sweep all before it, but disintegrated within a year. Next came Queens Park Rangers followed by Barcelona where he was an instant hit. He was eventually drawn back to England and Tottenham Hotspur before being offered the game's top job.

Venables has always known what he wants to do with a football team; he knows how players work, and whether you agree or disagree with him, his philosophy is clear. 'It's all very well to get the result, but to get the result well is the difficult thing,' he said. 'You can always do it the way teams like Norway do; be stubborn and occasionally break and get a goal, which is OK. You can't knock it but who wants to watch it?' A statement of intent, but the way the national side works – players pulled from their clubs every now and again, a few days training to a different style and then out to do their best for their country – is not conducive to success. Venables wanted and needed more time – and he got it.

'I do feel coaching players for two days every five weeks is not enough, and that I could be helping players a great deal more,' he said. 'I've been criticized in the past for trying to do too much so I've got to recognize the parameters of the job and stick to them.

'It's frustrating because I get such a buzz out of working with players and building up to and playing the game – then they all leave and you're left planning again. If it sounds like a cushy number, then I tell you it's not because the pressure building up to a game is like nothing else I've experienced.'

The first match was at home to Denmark – the reigning European Champions at the time. A crowd of 71,000, excited by the potential of Venables' new England, turned up to watch a 1-0 home win – the goal coming from skipper David Platt.

Bit by bit, Venables drew the strands together, and his record from the first ten games was impressive. But better still was the way his England were playing. Crucially, Venables was respected by his players, and his skills as a communicator were paramount in getting his message across. Inventive – just check out the variations a Venables side will try with a free-kick – and understood, Venables was always asking questions, always looking at new ways to play the game and at the progress of other teams. He is also a hard but fair taskmaster, a man able to relate to his players. He knows enough to spot their weaknesses and can work on improving them – something that even the best internationals seize upon eagerly.

The record speaks for itself: ten played, five wins, four draws and one loss – to world champions Brazil. Even in that defeat England had performed well and were undone by some clinical finishing by their opponents.

Venables had forced a style on his England that was liked, that was within the capabilities of his players, and because of this they enjoyed their football. It showed in their attitude and in the way they performed on the pitch.

England continued to progress as Euro '96 drew nearer and nearer and, by the time the tournament arrived, expectations were not fuelled by jingoism but by a very real belief that the team and the country could do well. By this stage, Venables had announced that at the end of the competition he would step down as coach.

The hype was not to prove unfounded and Venables had instilled pride in his squad based on his own experiences – he won England caps at all levels. 'I remember very clearly the day I was picked, it felt wonderful – it meant everything,' he said. 'It was why you played in the park and all the hard work throughout your career was justified.'

His Euro '96 squad were to behave in the same way. 'Players should be delighted to be in the squad regardless of whether they are in the team – once in, the players should not need praise from me, I've shown them what I think.

'Togetherness is very important, Brazil link arms during penalty shoot-outs and I like that. They are saying there is no selfishness here. If I am in the team, fine. If not, we are still together. I am not unhappy. The cause is the thing and we care.'

England reached the semi-finals of Euro '96, where all that separated them from the Final was a penalty shoot-out won by the indefatigable Germans. But the most significant achievement of Venables' 23-match reign (one game against the Republic of Ireland in Dublin in February 1995 was abandoned after 27 minutes because of crowd trouble with England 1-0 down at the time) was the Euro '96 drubbing of Holland.

On that Wembley night England took apart a world-class side, led 4-0 and eventually won 4-1, with a performance that was as positive as it was skilful. It was a sure sign that England were a power again and a fine legacy for Venables to leave his successor. For once an England coach walked away from the job with his head held high, his self-esteem intact – the worries of the job had not left him in ruins.

For the Football Association it was time to send for Jimmy Armfield again.

And once again some of those familiar names were bandied about: Coppell and Keegan along with Manchester United boss Alex Ferguson, Howard Kendall, Bryan Robson and Howard Wilkinson. Some nominations were the product of imaginative speculation and as before, the retreat was sounded by those who were serious contenders.

Finally Hoddle emerged from the pack. Chelsea were eager to keep him, but with just a month on his contract to run at Stamford Bridge it quickly became clear that just as Venables had been the one real candidate in 1994, so Hoddle was the only real option in 1996.

The deal was done, Chelsea let him go and appointed Ruud Gullit in his place. Hoddle said: 'I've had a burning ambition to do this since I was very young. It's the only job in England, or abroad, which I could have left Chelsea for.'

Hoddle won 53 caps for England but should have won more. The complete footballer, he often found himself out of sorts with the England management. After a playing career that spanned Tottenham and Monaco, then Swindon Town and Chelsea – as a player-manager for both clubs – he was now in a position to call the shots.

As with the appointment of Venables, England had a coach trusted implicitly by the players. Here was a man who had played the game at the highest level, had been a real footballing artist. On top of that, he was taking over a squad that was on a high – confident and focused. But while Venables had started knowing his side were playing in the European Championship, Hoddle had the task of qualifying for the 1998 World Cup in France. It was a difficult starting point.

England were drawn in Group Two with Italy, Poland, Georgia and Moldova and Hoddle started off with a busy fixture list that took him to the known and the unknown. Italy and Poland had a history of causing England problems, while Georgia and Moldova were new nations to the competition. Even so, many a national manager – as history shows – has stumbled and fallen when faced with such opponents.

To make matters worse, Hoddle's very first game in charge was going to be a World Cup qualifier, away in Moldova. There was little room for manoeuvre but at least the foundations were solid and England made the best possible start – winning 3-0 with an assured performance.

Slowly Hoddle has been able to make his mark on the side. The team has moved forward and been blessed by a supply of supremely talented youngsters – a seemingly endless stream coming from Manchester United – who have settled into the national side with ease.

Like Venables, Hoddle had a terrific first ten matches to start his reign: nine wins and one defeat. It means that Hoddle can not only build up his squad's confidence with sweet talk that they are world-beaters – but he can also dig out the record book and show them that they can more than mix it with the best. Strange that with Venables and Hoddle there was an air of forced marriage about their appointment to the England job. Stranger still that it should seem such a perfect match.

The World Cup charge is definitely on....

ENGLAND MANAGERS

1946–62 Walter Winterbottom (P139, W78, D33, L28)
1963–74 Sir Alf Ramsey (P113, W69, D27, L17)
1974 Joe Mercer (caretaker) (P7, W3, D3, L1)
1974–77 Don Revie (P29, W14, D8, L7)
1977–82 Ron Greenwood (P55, W33, D12, L10)
1982–90 Bobby Robson (P95, W47, D30, L18)
1990–93 Graham Taylor (P38, W18, D13, L7)
1994–96 Terry Venables (P23 W11, D11, L1)
1996–present Glenn Hoddle

The Long and Winding Road to France

The World Cup throws up opportunities for exotic and far-flung adventures, but for every trek into remote and magical regions come several of the more earthbound variety. Keeping the concentration while all around the significance of football seems dramatically lessened by severe local hardship and the echo of global problems, requires a special kind of mental hardness. And so England headed into the unknown of Moldova. Still sore and wounded from memories of failing to make it to the 1994 World Cup in the USA, the journey was taken under the guidance of new coach, Glenn Hoddle. Misery of 1994, joy of 1990 when England made the semi-finals, now the route to 1998 needed some navigating. A wrong result could lead to a wrong turn on the road to France and a trip to World Cup oblivion. So with that in mind, England began the campaign in Moldova in September 1996.

1 September 1996 – Chisinau
MOLDOVA 0 ENGLAND 3

'THE GOOD THING was that we showed we had a cutting edge in the last third of the pitch.' **Glenn Hoddle**

A COUNTRY just five years old and found in the armpit of what was once the USSR, Moldova could

boast just 85 clubs and 8,000 players, but ever since David slew Goliath the big 'uns have never taken much comfort in such statistics.

There were 750 England fans – who paid £259 for a day-trip to Moldova – in the crowd of 15,000 in Chisinau, and the visitors discovered that their worst fears for the place were unfounded, as they took their places against the backdrop of the sinking sun. The early exchanges were as expected. England a touch hesitant, Moldova full of vim and vigour in attack but looking less than solid at the back – highlighted by a sixth-minute attack which ended with Paul Gascoigne cheated of rounding-off a simple chance because of a lack of inches in height.

Any uncertainties in the England midfield and defence were soothed by a double dose of goals. The first came in the 23rd minute when David Beckham sent Andy Hinchcliffe on the gallop down the left. His cross found Gary Neville and he played the ball back for Nick Barmby to hammer home.

Two minutes later, and barring a disaster of Hollywood proportions, England had the three points in the bag. Paul Ince charged forward, played a one-two with Barmby and put in a cross which Gascoigne looped into the net. Moldova continued to work hard and by half-time David Seaman was looking back on some near misses. Both Alexandru Popovic and Iuri Mitereu went close on several occasions.

It was a more settled England in the second half and Neville linked up with Gareth Southgate to provide new captain Alan Shearer with the third goal – his 11th in international football. Still Moldova poured forward and nearly scored a consolation goal when Stuart Pearce was said to have handled with three minutes of the match remaining. Ion Testimitanu smashed his kick against the bar and England were off to a flier.

Moldova: Romanenco, Secu, Nani, Testimitanu, Galdamasiuc, Epureanu, Curteanu, Belous (Sischin 58), Clescenco, Mitereu (Rebeja 61), Popovic.
England (3-5-2): Seaman, Southgate, Pallister, Pearce, G. Neville, Beckham, Ince, Gascoigne (Batty 80), Hinchcliffe, Barmby (Le Tissier 80), Shearer.
Subs not used: Walker, Campbell, Draper, Stone, Ferdinand.
England bookings: Pearce, Ince. **Scorers:** Barmby (23) 0-1, Gascoigne (25) 0-2, Shearer (61) 0-3. **Referee:** I. Koho (Finland). **Attendance:** 15,000.

9 October 1996 – Wembley

ENGLAND 2 POLAND 1

'IF WE ARE GOING TO DO WELL then a certain amount of sacrifice is required from myself, the players and everyone. You cannot do it without that sort of dedication.'
Glenn Hoddle

TENSE – there was no other way to describe England as they faced a Poland side apparently ripe for the plucking.

The Poles, who were supposed to be divided by feuds in their camp, had a miserable recent record and were expected to defend with all 11 men behind the ball. England, on the other hand, were invigorated by a long training camp and were ready to pick up the flag carried so splendidly throughout Euro '96.

The beauty of football is that nothing should be taken for granted. Six minutes into the match Poland were ahead. Worse for England, they were buzzing. Henryk Baluszynski broke for the right by-line, put in a cross that Krzysztof Warzycha deflected past a flat-footed Gary Neville, and Marek Citko controlled the ball before smashing it past David Seaman for his first international goal.

There were more scares to come. Seaman was left patrolling a penalty box guarded by hesitant defenders, but slowly England got a grip. Alan Shearer, leading from the front, was the man to put a nation's hopes back on track.

David Beckham found some space on the right and put in an early deep cross. Andrzej Wozinak came

out of the goal to try and collect the ball, but Shearer leapt fearlessly for the ball and just beat the goalkeeper to it, sending it into the net.

England went ahead 12 minutes later when Shearer and his Newcastle club-mate at the time, Les Ferdinand, brought their domestic understanding into play. Shearer received the ball from Ferdinand, went right and shot. The ball cannoned off a defender back to Ferdinand and he held it up before setting up the shot for Shearer. From then until half-time England were in the ascendancy, but a reorganized Poland defence saw the visitors begin the second half in determined and solid style. Seaman was called on to make a number of good saves as the match became very open.

England had a few chances to extend their lead but in the end, when the whistle went to signify the home win, it was greeted by relieved cheers.

England (3-5-2): Seaman, G. Neville, Southgate (Pallister 51), Pearce, Beckham, Ince, Gascoigne, Hinchcliffe, McManaman, Ferdinand, Shearer. **Subs not used:** Campbell, Platt, Le Tissier, Sheringham, Barmby, Walker. 2-1. **Poland:** Wozinak, Wojtala, Zielinski, Jozwiak, Hajto, Michaelski, Waldoch, Baluszynski, Nowak, Warzycha (Saganowski 75), Citko. **England bookings:** none. **Scorers:** Citko (6) 0-1; Shearer (25) 1-1; Shearer (37) **Referee:** H. Krug (Germany). **Attendance:** 74,663.

9 November 1996 – Tbilisi
GEORGIA 0 ENGLAND 2

'THERE ARE PRINCIPLES and disciplines you need in a team. They veered away from those against Poland, which meant we made it a harder night for ourselves than it should have been. Today was the opposite. As a collective performance it was tremendous.' **Glenn Hoddle.**

AGAINST a Georgia side expected to present a formidable challenge, England played with skill and considerable composure to achieve an impressive 2-0 victory. This was a team effort from the back through to the front, and so well-marshalled were the players that David Seaman hardly had a shot to save.

At the other end, Teddy Sheringham and Les Ferdinand formed a potent partnership which brought rewards as early as the 15th minute. Paul Gascoigne played the ball through for Ferdinand and he looked up and saw Sheringham moving into space on the right. Ferdinand delivered and Sheringham allowed his marker Murtaz Sheila to try but fail to make the interception before he was in on goal, scoring with a shot which came off a defender and went over the Georgia goalkeeper Irakli Zoidze.

England were out of sight before half-time. On this occasion they adopted the direct approach. Tony Adams made the interception, Gascoigne and Sheringham took the ball upfield before releasing

Ferdinand for a run on goal. He shot home from just one yard inside the penalty area.

With Adams, Campbell and Southgate solid at the back, the feared raids of Georgi Kinkladze, known to England fans through his scintillating play at Manchester City, failed to materialize.

Instead it was England, working their socks off, who had the play. David Batty and Paul Ince worked like Trojans in midfield while Gascoigne too was called on to run and run. The Georgians were surprisingly devoid of attacking ploys and by the final whistle England had not only progressed through points won, but had also made a huge mental leap as a side of quality coming good.

Georgia: Zoidze, Lobjanidze, Tskhadadze, Sheila, Gogichaishvili, Nemsadze, Jamarauli, Kinkladze, Kobiashvili (Ghudushauri 67), Arveladze (Gogrichiani 52), Ketsbaia.
England (3-5-2): Seaman, Campbell, Southgate, Adams, Beckham, Batty, Ince, Gascoigne, Hinchcliffe, Sheringham, Ferdinand (Wright 81).
Subs not used: G. Neville, Pearce, Platt, McManaman, Le Tissier, Walker.
Scorers: Sheringham (15) 0-1; Ferdinand (37) 0-2. **England bookings:** Beckham.
Referee: J. Monteiro. **Attendance:** 48,000.

12 February 1997 – Wembley
ENGLAND 0 ITALY 1

'OF COURSE IT'S A DISAPPOINTMENT – but it's not a disaster. There's a lot more football to be played. There is no way we are out of this World Cup competition.' **Glenn Hoddle.**

NOT just a big match – a huge match. England and Italy had been neck-and-neck in Group Two, with England holding a slight advantage having played and

won three matches to two played and won by Italy. Already it was clear that by October 1997 the group winners, and the only out-and-out qualifiers for finishing top of the table, would be one of these two.

Italy, finalists four years earlier, and with a number of their star players earning a living in the Premiership, arrived knowing that they faced an England side that had never lost a World Cup match on home soil.

One of the main dangers to England was going to be the power and precision of Italy's dead-ball play. Give a free-kick to the Italians within shooting range and the likes of Alessandro del Piero and Gianfranco Zola could cause mayhem.

In the event, del Piero only made the substitutes' bench, but England's luck was out as David Seaman was forced out of the game because of a knee injury and Tony Adams also withdrew. That left Ian Walker in goal with Gary Neville, Stuart Pearce and Sol Campbell forming the backline. The midfield included Steve McManaman and Matt Le Tissier, and although both players showed some early promise, Wembley stadium fell silent after just 18 minutes and it was a case of the classic counter-attack.

Pearce led a charge down the left and played the ball to Le Tissier. He was caught in possession. Alessandro Costacurta pounced and fed the ball forward down the inside-right channel, where Zola picked it up. He moved forward into the penalty box and from a tight angle and, despite Campbell's arrival, fired a shot past Walker on his near post.

England sparked now and again, David Beckham stinging the hands of Angelo Peruzzi with one free-kick and Le Tissier putting a good heading chance wide, but it was Italy who posed the sharpest threat and the final tally of shots, which had England making four for every one by the visitors, was misleading.

Demetrio Albertini, the AC Milan player, had an increasing influence as the Italians used possession wisely, and the knowledge that Italy never waste a lead seemed to add an air of desperation to England's efforts.

Hoddle threw on Les Ferdinand for Le Tissier, Paul Merson for McManaman and Ian Wright for David Batty, and while the tempo did pick up, there seemed little chance of England preserving that proud home record. On a cold February night, England's route to France had been hit by roadworks.

England (3-5-2): Walker, G. Neville, Campbell, Pearce, Beckham, Batty (Wright 87), Ince, Le Saux, McManaman (Merson 76), Le Tissier (Ferdinand 60), Shearer. **Subs not used:** Southgate, James, Lee, Redknapp.
Italy: Peruzzi, Ferrara, Costacurta, Cannavaro, Di Livio, Di Matteo, Albertini, D. Baggio, Maldini, Zola (Fuser 90), Casiraghi (Ravanelli 76).
Scorers: Zola (18) 0-1. **England bookings:** none. **Referee:** S. Puhl (Hungary).
Attendance: 75,055.

30 April 1997 – Wembley
ENGLAND 2 GEORGIA 0

'PEOPLE TALK ABOUT THE BEAUTIFUL GAME and I would love to play it. But it's not like that in the modern era.' **Glenn Hoddle.**

EARLIER in the month Italy drew 0-0 in Poland, which meant that their advantage over England was two points with the same number of games played. And as England prepared for Georgia, Italy were playing the return leg against Poland in Naples.

The incentive was to keep up with the Italians and at the same time repair some of the damage done by that February defeat. England were bolstered by the return of both Tony Adams and David Seaman, but the performance turned in was one of functional English-battling quality rather than anything blessed with finesse or inspiration.

As expected, England made the early running, with Teddy Sheringham and Alan Shearer working hard to make a hole in the red ranks of the Georgia

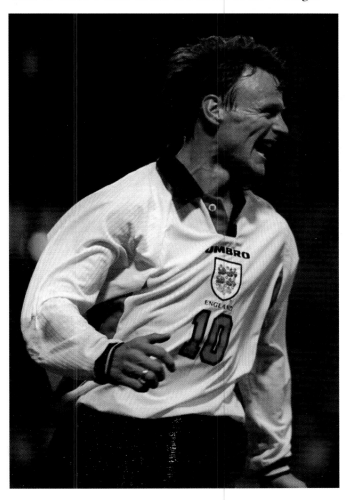

defence, constantly looking to pull markers out of position. In midfield David Batty was rock solid and penetrating with his passing.

In defence, Sol Campbell had his sharpest game yet for England, constantly alert to the rare dangers posed by Georgia. The sole creator in the England ranks was David Beckham; but in the early stages there was too much puff and not enough penetration.

Robert Lee nearly made a breakthrough when he hit the post with a lofted shot and Sheringham squandered a free header. Half-time was looming, Italy were ahead in Poland and England were struggling.

But then it clicked. Graeme Le Saux played the ball down the left to Shearer. He chested it down, thumped in a centre and there was Sheringham, ahead of his marker, Murtaz Sheila, to head home. It was the perfect time to score, but curiously it was the Georgians who came out in the second half looking more eager for the fray. They would have been level had Seaman not stretched out a right leg to deny Gocha Gogrichiani.

Beckham continued to offer occasional glimpses of a breakthrough, but still England needed a second goal to ease their very visible nerves. It finally came in the last minute. An indirect free-kick close in but from a tight angle saw Sheringham roll the ball back and there was Shearer to thunder home a shot with vicious venom.

England (3-5-2): Seaman, G. Neville, Adams (Southgate 87), Campbell, Beckham, Ince (Redknapp 77), Batty, Lee, Le Saux, Sheringham, Shearer. **Subs not used:** Flowers, P. Neville, McManaman, Fowler, L. Ferdinand. **Georgia:** Zoidze, Tskhadadze, Chikhradze, Sheqiladze, Sheila, Machaviariani (Gogrichiani 32, A. Arveladze 76), Jamarauli, Nemsadze, Ketsbaia, Kinkladze (Gakhokidze 62), S. Arveladze. **Scorers:** Sheringham (43) 1-0, Shearer (90) 2-0. **England bookings:** Le Saux, Lee. **Referee:** R. Harrel (France). **Attendance:** 71,208.

31 May 1997 – Chorzow
POLAND 0 ENGLAND 2

'I WAS KICKED A LOT but I had the last laugh, I thoroughly enjoy that kind of thing. I take it as a challenge and a sign of respect.' **Alan Shearer.**

AT the very least a win in Poland would assure England of a place in the World Cup qualifying play-offs, at best it could be the springboard to a greater showdown with Italy in October. All well and good, but Poland is a cold and inhospitable place, as past England experiences prove only too well. On top of this, if Poland won, they still had an outside chance of being there in France. So here was a game with two sides having it all to play for. First blood would go a long way to dictating the course of the action.

It was England who struck first with a peach of a goal. Paul Ince – labelled a 'headless chicken' when England last lost their way in a World Cup qualifying match in Poland – was the inspiration. Ince made a powerful foray forward and there was Shearer to snap up the incisive pass to score.

England settled back to their rigid formation, prepared to let the Poles, as the home team, take up the responsibility for attacking while ready to seize any counter-attacking chances that came their way. It looked good, with a strong spine holding up England's more fancy parts.

David Seaman, Gareth Southgate, Ince and Shearer were the backbone of the side, while Teddy Sheringham, Sol Campbell, David Beckham and Graeme Le Saux brought confident craft to the team. The only scares came in the closing minutes of the first half as Poland turned up the heat.

There was even room for England to win a penalty and waste it as Shearer missed, before a swift counter-attack, designed by Robert Lee, with the finish delivered by Sheringham in the last minute, sealed one of England's most satisfying wins in qualifying.

Not only had England played well, but the players had held their nerve and their shape and, better still, refused to be intimidated by a Poland side that played it rougher and rougher as the minutes slipped by.

For England, the victory brought that October date in Rome with Italy into even sharper focus. It also brought about the possibility of automatic qualification for France by virtue of being the best of the runner-up finishers in Europe, a fact that gave the whole campaign a significant boost. Beckoning after Poland was the Tournoi de France – a four-way event featuring some of the top sides in the world: Italy, France, Brazil and England. It was to be Hoddle's team who won.

England (3-5-2): Seaman, G. Neville, Southgate, Campbell, Beckham (P. Neville 89), Lee, Ince, Gascoigne (Batty 17), Le Saux, Sheringham, Shearer. **Subs not used:** Flowers, Pearce, Keown, Scholes, Wright. **Poland:** Wozinak, Kalunzy, Zielinski, Jozwiak, Ledwon, Bukalski (Swierczewksi 45), Waldoch, Nowak (Kucharski 57), Majak, Dembinski, Juskowiak (Adamczyk 51). **Scorers:** Shearer (6) 0-1, Sheringham (90) 0-2 **England bookings:** Ince, Batty. **Referee:** U. Meier (Switzerland). **Attendance:** 35,000.

10 September 1997 – Wembley
ENGLAND 4 MOLDOVA 0

'EVERYONE EXPECTED us to go to Rome needing to win but now psychologically, the pressure in Rome will be on the Italians.' **Glenn Hoddle**

IT was a very good night in England – the biggest win in the group stages of qualifying for France was achieved while Italy were relinquishing their two-point lead in the table by drawing 0-0 in Georgia. It meant that all England needed in a month's time in

Rome was a draw. Better still, the progress made since the summer was gathering greater momentum. After the Poland win had come a successful Tournoi de France, which hinted that England were turning into a real world footballing force.

The solid spine of the side, running through the middle but now missing Alan Shearer who had been injured playing for Newcastle in a pre-season match, was holding firm, with growing confidence which allowed the players away from the core to turn in ever more heartening performances.

This Wembley night it was the turn of Paul Gascoigne to be the maestro, the innovator and ultimately the ruthless destroyer. Moldova could not

handle him – but then on the form he was showing that night, very few defenders could have coped. Aiding and abetting him were Arsenal's Ian Wright and Manchester United's Paul Scholes. Both were excellent. It was Scholes who scored first, thanks to a pinpoint cross from David Beckham. Scholes dived forward and the ball was in the back of the net.

With David Batty solid in midfield, it allowed Gascoigne to motor up and down and Scholes to buzz. Gareth Southgate was holding the back but moving up into midfield to plug any gaps. Hoddle's tactical reading of the match was working a treat. A minute into the second half and England were moving out of Moldova's sight. Gascoigne was fed by Wright, who foraged forward while Gascoigne ran at a retreating defence before feeding the ball back to Wright and it was 2-0.

Stuart Ripley came on for Beckham and he almost immediately sent in a cross that Gascoigne put against the post, and Batty missed in the follow-through. There were, however, still more goals in England and it was Wright who was the provider as he played-in Gascoigne with a neat one-two.

Wright was not done, however. When Stan Collymore pushed the ball forward in the final minute, the Arsenal striker was on it in a flash and striding towards goal for his second of the match and England's fourth. The night finished with the news that Italy had only managed a draw in Georgia and England were top of the group. Suddenly a night in Rome could not come quickly enough.

England (3-5-2): Seaman, G. Neville, Southgate, Campbell, Beckham (Ripley 57, Butt 75), Batty, Gascoigne, P. Neville, Scholes, Ferdinand (Collymore 82), Wright.
Subs not used: Walker, Pallister, Le Saux, Lee. **England bookings:** Campbell.
Moldova: Romanenco, Stroenco, Fistican, Testimitanu, Spinu, Shishkin (Popovici 60), Curteanu, Culibaba (Suharev 52), Rebeja, Mitereu, Rogaciov (Cibotari 74).
Scorers: Scholes (29) 1-0, Wright (46) 2-0, Gascoigne (80) 3-0, Wright (89) 4-0. **Referee:** K-E Nilsson (Sweden). **Attendance:** 74,102.

11 October 1997 – Rome
ITALY 0 ENGLAND 0

'AS A COACH you get a massive pat on the back or a massive knife in the back.' **Glenn Hoddle**

WHEN in Rome ... do as England did if you want World Cup success.

Italy had to win, otherwise they would face a detour and a play-off to secure a place in France, while for England a draw would send them straight to the finals. Incentive enough for both sides to make this

some match. And while the action on the field was not thrilling in terms of purist football, there was enough quality on show to please the sternest of critics, and a sweaty tension to send hearts beating fast.

This was a tactical confrontation *par excellence*. Glenn Hoddle v Cesare Maldini. Maldini had won a battle at Wembley but now it was the whole war and, against Maldini's better nature, his team had to go out and force the pace.

England, deploying Tony Adams, Gareth Southgate and Sol Campbell across the back, were well-marshalled and unyielding. In the middle David Batty was refusing to be moved, playing with authority and a look of determination that said he was not going

to be provoked into anything by anybody. Next to him was the fearless and bloody Paul Ince, who disappeared from the fray to have stitches in a head wound, returning later, white shirt stained pink with his blood.

The attack consisted of Ian Wright ploughing a lone furrow, but not for a minute did he stop running as he moved this way and that, whenever the England midfield had the ball. Wright's job was to distract the Italian defence and he did that to perfection.

So what of the chances? This was never going to be a goal feast and there were no real clear-cut chances until the last, heart-stopping minute. The Italians had poured forward in numbers when Ian Wright was set free. He galloped past the defence and rounded Angelo Peruzzi, but from the ever-narrowing angle could only hit the post. The ball rebounded but Sheringham failed to get a shot in.

As swiftly as England had counter-attacked, Italy struck back and a cross from the right found Christian Vieri's head, he had to score. The ball, however, flashed wide.

Full-time and England were in France and Italy on the road to Moscow for a second attempt at qualifying. Composure, commitment and great skill had brought England through in a situation that was as testing as anything they are likely to face in France in the summer of 1998.

Italy: Peruzzi, Nesta, Costacurta, Cannavaro, Maldini (Benarrivo 31), Di Livio, D. Baggio, Albertini, Zola (Del Piero 64), Inzaghi (Chiesa 45), Vieri.
England (3-5-2): Seaman, Beckham, Campbell, Adams, Southgate, Le Saux, Ince, Gascoigne (Butt 88), Batty, Sheringham, Wright.
Subs not used: G. Neville, Walker, P. Neville, McManaman, Scholes, Fowler.
Referee: M. Van Der Ende (Holland). **Attendance:** 81,200.

The Greatest Show on Earth

LITTLE ACORNS – MIGHTY OAKS

In the beginning there were 13 invited teams – some grateful guests, others cajoled and threatened – but there were enough to make a competition of it and Uruguay, the hosts celebrating the 100th year of their independence, won.

Now, 68 years on for France '98, the 13 have grown to a staggering 172 all wanting to be there. They have to be whittled down by the five world-wide federations to a manageable 32 – and even that figure is the most yet for the finals stage of the World Cup.

Every World Cup cycle has seen the number of nations wanting to compete grow – with one exception – and 1978 was the watershed year when the number taking part broke the three-figure barrier as 106 nations tried to reach Argentina. There folllowed 109 for Spain in 1982, 121 for Mexico in 1986, 112 for Italy in 1990 then 144 in the USA in 1994.

As the numbers of the wannabes climb higher, so the figures for the 'been there, done it' brigade stay constant. There have been only six winners over the years and all of them – bar England – have carried away the trophy more than once. Only ten nations, in various permutations, have contested the Final.

Down the years the World Cup has reflected the changing world, nations have come and gone, great powers like the USSR have fractured and become multiple countries; Ukraine, Belarus, Estonia, Latvia, Georgia, to name but a few of the pieces left by the fallout. New awareness and new territories have created other challengers. China now has real pretensions when it comes to the World Cup and although they failed to qualify this time, there is no doubt they'll be back.

The biggest expectations, however, are for one of the African nations. When Cameroon made the 1982 finals in Spain they were just another exotic outsider, there to make up the numbers. Eight years later they were back – proving to be far more than just day-trippers. They beat the World Cup holders Argentina 1-0 in the tournament's opening game and then just went on and on.

In the group stages they beat Romania 2-1 and were through to the last 16. On they marched, scoring a thrilling extra-time win over Colombia for a quarter-final spot against England. England, the country that gave football to the world, needed extra-time to see off the challenge of the vibrant and colourful Africans.

Even then victory came courtesy of a huge helping of luck. England went ahead, Cameroon levelled the match and then took the lead. Time was running out and England were looking to be in desperate trouble when Gary Lineker burst into the Cameroon penalty area and was fouled. He got up to score from the spot and was to do exactly the same in extra-time. But Cameroon might well have sprung a major shock.

And that is the beauty of the World Cup – surprises are always possible. Back in 1966, the men from

North Korea knocked Italy out thanks to a 1-0 group win and then were 3-0 up against Portugal in the quarter-final before being beaten 5-3. Magic, romance and eye-rubbing 'I can't believe it' stuff.

And so to France. Africa is the quarter from which the surprises are expected. Cameroon may be a little past their sell-by date, but the real threat could be posed by Nigeria – the Olympic football champions. The World Cup is littered with great sides that have evolved from Olympic teams – like the Hungary of the Mighty Magyars in the 1950s, unbeaten between 1951 and 1956 except for the World Cup Final of 1954, when they lost 3-2 to West Germany in Berne.

Then the established teams will take some shifting. South American sides might have a reputation for not doing too well in World Cups in Europe, but few can expect a Brazilian side that includes Romário and Ronaldo to fold that easily. Brazil are the proud holders of the cup, the only side to have won it four times and they are desperate to win it again.

Germany – once successful West Germany and less successful East Germany – another nation changed by political history and unified, are almost certain to pose a threat. Even when the side is not glittering with talent, it has a frighteningly functional approach that has been a proven winner time and again. Germany are the current European Champions and will be hard to beat.

Holland have the players of flair and style, as well as the tendency to have a tantrum. If all is well they will be a dangerous side, as will the Italians who were forced into the ignominy of a play-off game against Russia to make it in the first place.

A host nation has not won the World Cup for 20 years – when Argentina beat Holland 3-1 in Buenos Aires – but then Spain, Mexico and the USA, three of the next four host countries, do not have the greatest of World Cup traditions even if they have sparkled on occasions.

This time France look a strong side. They won their only major international trophy at home in the European Championship of 1984, when Michel Platini led France to beat Spain in the Final, and that will be seen as an omen. Their players are scattered around Europe, playing for the best teams in Italy, Spain and England, and they have the flair to do well.

England, too, are a side coming into form. Young and benefitting from the influx of top overseas players into the Premier League, which in turn has raised the standard, their ambitions are built upon real foundations.

As the number of contestants to the finals has grown, so too has the coverage, the spin-offs from the

competition, the merchandise. More matches than ever in France will in turn lead to the highest ever number of spectators attending live games – and the television viewing figures will be astronomical. From the middle of the hottest desert to the heart of the coldest ice cap, televisions will be tuned to the greatest show on earth – it is some claim to make, but as the past has proved and the future leads us to expect, the World Cup is just that.

The Growth
of the World Cup

1930

THE IDEA WAS BRILLIANT – but selling it was a completely different matter. It started with just 13 teams and came about after plenty of wheeling and dealing in the corridors outside committee rooms and many hours of heated discussions and angry exchanges within. Yet to have got 13 teams, an agreed host nation and the organization in place was a minor miracle considering the strangulated gestation of the idea. Today the World Cup is the single greatest sporting event – growing with every turn of its four-year cycle.

The brainchild of two Frenchmen, Jules Rimet and Henri Delaunay, the idea was conceived in 1904 at the first meeting of FIFA, but it was to be another 16 years (at the Olympic Games in Antwerp in 1920) before the movement began to gain momentum.

One of the major problems was that the British football associations – the ones responsible for giving the world the game of football and then introducing a formalized structure for it – were suspicious of the whole FIFA concept. Here was a global body formed by seven European nations, three of them without their own national football associations. On top of that, France had only played their first international 20 days before the meeting, something that three other countries at the meeting – Spain, Denmark and Switzerland – were yet to do.

Not wishing to seem churlish, the British joined – but then withdrew in 1928, angry at the way the demarcation lines between amateur and professional were being blurred. This was a problem the British

had settled back in 1883, but in Europe and South America 'broken time' payments (money paid to players for time off work) were either openly allowed or paid discreetly, allowing the players concerned to keep their amateur status. British objections at this point centred around the Olympic Games football tournament – the only world championship of any kind and one which the British felt should adhere strictly to the amateur ethos.

And so, on 26 May 1928, the first World Cup started to take shape without England, Wales, Scotland and Ireland. FIFA, presided over by Rimet, announced the competition and offered an open invite to the footballing nations of the world.

Next, a host country had to be found. FIFA met on 18 May 1929 to consider the claims of Italy, Holland, Spain, Sweden and Uruguay. It was the South American country which made the most passionate pitch – 1930 was the centenary of their independence and they pledged to build a new stadium for the competition. Perhaps the most persuasive argument of all, however, was the promise to foot the bill for the other participating nations.

Uruguay got the nod, whereupon Austria, Czechoslovakia, Germany and Switzerland said they were not going – South America was too far away (three weeks by boat). Tit for tat, the South American nations threatened to quit FIFA because of the snub and another compromise had to be thrashed out.

Belgium, France, Romania and Yugoslavia were persuaded to go and take up the challenge of Argentina, Bolivia, Brazil, Chile, Mexico, Paraguay, the USA (then made up of former English and Scottish

professionals), Peru and of course the host nation.

The Belgians, French and Romanians set sail on the *Conte Verde* on 21 June 1930 and on the Sunday afternoon of 13 July 1930 France and Mexico played the first-ever World Cup match. There was controversy when, ten minutes into the game, the French goalkeeper Alex Thépot took a kick in the jaw and had to leave the field. This was in the days before substitutes, but even so the French triumphed 4-1. Yet they failed to make the semi-finals after another controversial match — a 1-0 defeat by Argentina in a game that ended six minutes early when the referee blew up for full-time just as France seemed poised to equalize. In a contest structured so that it pitched together the winners from the four groups, Argentina, Yugoslavia, the USA and Uruguay remained.

The USA had not conceded a goal in the tournament, but were swept away 6-1 by Argentina and the other semi-final showed an equally high score as Yugoslavia were trounced 6-1 by Uruguay.

And so to the Centenario Stadium in Montevideo, filled to its 100,000 capacity for Uruguay against Argentina — to be played on 17 July, Uruguay's Independence day. These two countries were bitter rivals and an endless procession of boats had crossed the River Plate from Buenos Aires to Montevideo, the Argentines chanting 'Victory or Death'.

The match was 12 minutes old when Pablo Dorado put Uruguay ahead; but then Peucelle equalized and in the 37th minute, Stábile, the tournament's leading scorer with eight goals, made it 2-1 to Argentina with a goal the home crowd claimed was offside. At half-time the home fans wept and prayed. And those prayers were answered. Pedro Cea made it 2-2, then in the 68th minute Santos Iriarte put Uruguay ahead, leaving Castro to score the fourth in the closing seconds.

Jose Nasazzi stepped forward to collect the 30cm gold trophy, the 'Victoire aux auiles d'or' — sculpted by Frenchman Abel Lafleur — as Montevideo went mad. In Argentina, the Uruguayan embassy was stoned and the crowd cleared away only after the police opened fire. The World Cup had arrived.

1954

THE SECOND WORLD WAR had come and gone and the World Cup had been contested three more times since Uruguay triumphed in the first tournament — won by Italy in 1934, successfully defended by them in 1938 and then claimed again by Uruguay in 1950.

By the time the competition headed for Switzerland in 1954, there were 38 nations wanting to play in the tournament and this number had been whittled down to 16 — split into four groups of four. One of the problems had been the exact format of the finals, up to this point a strange mish-mash of straight knock-out matches and a league system with no designated Final. In Switzerland it was going to be straightforward, but even then a spanner was thrown into the works of simplicity.

There would be two seeded teams in each group and they would not face each other. That meant that each side played two group games and the weakest faced the strongest. Such a system was open to cynical calculation by the teams, as Germany in Group Two proved. The team they wanted to avoid was Brazil so they worked out that by losing to Hungary — they sent out a virtual reserve team and were beaten 8-3 — they then had to beat Turkey in a play-off match. They did so, winning 7-2 to earn a quarter-final match against Yugoslavia.

Yet the intricacies of the system should not cloud the beauty of the game and this special era. This was the age of the superb Hungarian side — the Mighty Magyars as the British press had dubbed them, a description that was unerring in its accuracy. This was the Hungary of Ferenc Puskás, Nandor Hidegkuti, Josef Bozsik, Sandor Kocsis and Zoltan Czibor. They were to lose only one match between 1950 and 1956 and could boast 6-3 and 7-1 wins over England. The tragedy was in the timing of that one defeat – but more of that later.

England, seeded in Group Four, drew 4-4 with Belgium and beat Switzerland 2-0 to earn a quarter-final with Uruguay, 7-0 conquerors of Scotland. Brazil reached the last eight, as did Switzerland via a play-off with Italy. Yet Hungary, who had faced Germany in a group match, had suffered a severe blow when Puskás had been deliberately kicked on the ankle by Werner Liebrich, the West German centre-half, and was left on the sidelines until the Final.

The Germans cantered through to the semi-finals after a 2-0 quarter-final win over Yugoslavia, but Hungary had the tough one – against Brazil. On paper it should have been a match of footballing magic, but the reality was very different as the two sides became embroiled in an infamous match known as 'The Battle of Berne'.

Hungary, in typical swirling, dazzling style, were 2-0 up in seven minutes, but a series of niggling fouls by the Hungarians lit a fuse. Two penalties, the first to Brazil and the second to Hungary in the 61st minute made it 3-1 but only succeeded in fanning the flames. Brazil clawed back to 3-2, then Bozsik and Nilton Santos of Brazil were at each other. The referee sent them off as already vicious tackles became down-right nasty. Hungary scored a fourth and won 4-2 but then the two sides became involved in a dressing-room brawl.

Meanwhile Austria won a finals epic, conquering Switzerland 7-5 in a match that had five goals in one ten-minute period, while Uruguay – yet to lose a match in the World Cup finals – came through 4-2 against England. The semi-finals were Germany against Austria and Hungary against Uruguay.

The muscular Germans powered past a technically superior Austria with a resounding 6-1 win while Hungary and Uruguay were involved in a titanic battle that still stands as one of the great games in World Cup history. Hungary were 2-0 up, but Uruguay would not give up and Juan Eduardo Hohberg levelled the scores. Extra-time was played and Uruguay, visibly tiring, were beaten 4-2. 'We beat the best team we ever met,' said Gyula Mandi, the Hungarian manager, graciously.

And so to the Final in Berne with Hungary the out-and-out favourites. Puskás came back, but the power of hindsight shows it to be the wrong decision. True to form Hungary were 2-0 up after eight minutes, Puskás scoring one of the goals, Czibor the other, yet the Germans would not roll over.

Inspired by the sensational goalkeeping of Toni Turek and the drive of Helmut Rahn, the Germans pulled back to 2-2 by half-time. Hungary, with Puskás struggling, were clearly unbalanced and the Germans could sense it. Five minutes remained when Rahn found himself with four defenders ahead of him; he made space and delivered the perfect shot. It was 3-2 to Germany.

Time was running out, but Hungary kept going. Puskás had the ball in the net but the goal was controversially disallowed for offside. Germany hung on for a 3-2 win and Hungary had lost one fateful match in an otherwise incredible six-year undefeated run.

They had earned the unwanted albatross of praise – the greatest team never to have won the World Cup.

1966

I N EURO '96 THE ENGLAND FANS sang about football coming home. It had, but not quite in the same way as it did in 1966 – a date of more historical significance to England football fans than 1066 and all that.

This was the year England hosted the tournament and it was the year they became only the fifth country to win the World Cup, making the most of home advantage. It had been decided that whoever won the Jules Rimet trophy for a third time would keep it forever and in 1966 Italy, Uruguay and Brazil

entered the competition with a chance of taking that honour.

Bigger and better than ever, there were 71 teams vying for a place in the finals, the holders Brazil and hosts England finally joined by 14 other sides, whittled down through the qualifying tournament. This brought the likes of North Korea and Portugal to the contest, and both these sides were to light up the show with some superb performances.

England opened with a 0-0 draw against Uruguay, but it was the 5-0 victory for West Germany over Switzerland in Group Two which rang the loudest warning bells. The shock was the demise of the defending champions Brazil.

They opened with a comfortable enough win over Bulgaria, scoring twice and conceding none, but in the course of the game Pelé was scythed down and forced to sit out the next match – against Hungary. And here it started to go wrong. Hungary won 3-1,

leaving the Brazilians needing a win from their last group match with Portugal. Inspired by Eusébio – one of the stars of 1966 – Portugal won 3-1; Brazil were out of the tournament and Pelé – back in the side but again singled out for some rough treatment – returned home vowing never to play in a World Cup again.

England, meanwhile, had beaten Mexico and France 2-0 to qualify for the quarter-finals, where they were joined by Uruguay. In Group Two Germany and Argentina went through, while Group Three provided Portugal and Hungary. The shock was in Group Four. The USSR were expected to progress but so too were the Italians.

Instead, playing North Korea at Ayresome Park – the former home of Middlesbrough – Park Doo-ik, an army dentist, scored the only goal of the game to send Italy home early. They met with a hostile reception at Genoa Airport, where they were pelted with rotten fruit – not so much 'just one cornetto' as a 'fistful of mouldy tomatoes'.

North Korea then faced Portugal in the quarter-final at Goodison Park and within 24 minutes were 3-0 up. However, they lacked experience on the international stage, did not know how to close the game down and Eusébio galvanized his side by scoring four goals in 34 minutes. In the end Eusébio – who was to finish the tournament top scorer with nine goals – had turned it around as Portugal won 5-3.

Germany thumped Uruguay 4-0 and the USSR won 2-1 against Hungary. That left England against Argentina to play out a game every bit as notorious as 'The Battle of Berne' between Brazil and Hungary in Switzerland in 1954.

It was clear that Argentina were technically a highly-skilled side, but their fatal flaw was their temperament. Poisoned by a vicious, cynical streak, the Argentine players fouled just about anything that moved, and the worst culprit was their captain Antonio Rattin. While all around him team-mates were being booked, Rattin continued to hack away, impervious to warnings from the referee.

Something had to give and it was the referee's patience. He sent Rattin off, but he refused to go and for 11 minutes the Argentine players argued the case, until eventually Rattin left. England won 1-0 but at the end Alf Ramsey ran on to the pitch to tell his players not to swap shirts with their opponents. He was to go on to call his rivals 'animals', although he later apologized for his remark.

Ramsey, appointed in 1962, was the first England manager to be given *carte blanche* with selection and his loyalty to his players was absolute. In the group match with France, Nobby Stiles had put in a crude tackle on a French player right beneath the Royal Box at Wembley where some of the FA hierarchy were sitting. They insisted that Ramsey should drop Stiles for the next match, but Ramsey was having none of it. He said he would rather resign.

Germany beat the USSR to reach the Final while two great goals from Bobby Charlton saw England past Portugal, both semi-finals ending 2-1.

It was to be a classic Final, still clouded today by controversy over England's third goal. Germany took first blood after 13 minutes; Helmut Haller pounced on Ray Wilson's poor clearance and bingo.

Geoff Hurst headed the equalizer from Bobby Moore's quick free-kick and then in the second half Hurst's West Ham colleague Peters added the second. England clung on, but in the dying moments of the game Weber scored Germany's second.

'You've beaten them once – now you've got to do it again,' said Ramsey as he geed up his men for extra-time. 'Look at them, they're finished.'

Indeed they were. Hurst, with his back to goal, swivelled and shot from Alan Ball's cross and the ball crashed against the bar then bounced down. Roger Hunt, following up, raised his arms in celebration and the referee, following confirmation from the Russian linesman Bakhramov, awarded the goal. Slow-motion film fails to prove conclusively one way or the other whether the ball had crossed the line, and even today Germans will argue that it did not.

Hurst, however, settled the issue with the last kick of the match, latching on to Moore's long clearance and blasting the ball home to become the first and to date the only man to score a hat-trick in a World Cup Final. Moore collected the trophy and England, home of the Swinging Sixties revolution, went into party mode.

1970

ENGLAND WENT TO MEXICO to defend their trophy, and they put up a brave fight – but this was a tournament to mark the return of Brazil to their brilliant best; a fitting finale for Pelé, still the world's greatest player, to strut for a final time on such a grand stage. It was also to mark the emergence of new stars.

Once again there were four groups of four teams, and in Group One the hosts Mexico finished behind the USSR to qualify for the quarter-finals. Group Two had Italy and Uruguay as qualifiers although Israel, eliminated in fourth place along with Sweden, had come away from their first finals with one defeat and two draws.

The real interest was in Group Three, where England and Brazil were together, along with Romania and Czechoslovakia. As soon as the groups became known, the clash between the defending champions and the soon-to-be crowned champions was billed as 'the real Final'. It was a match that lived up to all expectations. Alf Ramsey was still in charge and had the core of the England squad that had succeeded four years earlier, supplemented by talented newcomers such as Terry Cooper, Alan Mullery and Francis Lee. Brazil too had fresh faces: Jairzinho, Rivelino and Tostão.

Mexico in June is hot at the best of times, hot-ter still at noon – the scheduled time for the kick-off at the behest of the television companies. This meant temperatures of almost 100°F. On top of that, the England squad had hardly slept the previous night, kept awake by Brazilian fans who had surrounded the team's hotel to chant all night.

Yet England were worthy World Champions, mad dogs and Englishmen prepared to go out in the midday sun. The intent to hang on to their trophy was there for all to see after ten minutes. Jairzinho burst down the wing; Gordon Banks, the England goal-keeper, moved to his near post; the cross was whipped in as Pelé came storming into the middle of the penal-ty area, and he climbed majestically and powered his header down towards the far post. He was wheeling away yelling as Banks crossed his goal, twisted and turned in his dive – and forced the ball away for the greatest save ever.

There was nothing Banks could do in the sec-ond half, however, when Tostão launched the killer move, racing past three defenders, playing the ball on to Pelé who found Jairzinho and it was in the net. Jairzinho, though not the top scorer in Mexico, was to notch up a goal in every match Brazil played.

England stormed back and laid siege to the Brazilian goal, squandered a number of gilt edged chances and had to face a 1-0 defeat. The conse-quences of which were a quarter-final with the old foe, West Germany. Brazil were to go on and beat Peru 4-2, while Uruguay won 1-0 in extra-time against the USSR and Italy need-ed extra-time to con-quer Mexico 4-1.

Now came the England-Germany match. England suf-fered a blow when goalkeeper Gordon Banks had to with-draw because of food poisoning, thought to have been picked up from a bottle of beer. This meant Peter Bonetti took his place. Still, there was no panic for England. They led 1-0 at half-time thanks to an Alan Mullery goal, and were

1974

ahead 2-0 with just over 20 minutes to play after Martin Peters scored in the 50th minute.

Then – disaster. A Franz Beckenbauer shot squeezed under Bonetti's body and England started to flag. Ramsey played his substitutes' card, but changed the balance of his team and eight minutes from the end Uwe Seeler's header levelled the scores at 2-2. In extra-time there was only ever going to be one winner and it was Gerd Müller who wrapped it up, 3-2. Sweet revenge for Germany.

Already Mexico 1970 had served up a feast of football, but there was more to come in the pulsating semi-final between Italy and Germany. The Italians were following a tactic of defence as the only form of attack, being content to sneak a goal and soak up the pressure. They led 1-0 until Karl-Heinz Schnellinger scored in the third minute of injury time. Extra-time and the floodgates opened. Müller put the Germans ahead, the Italians scored twice before Müller levelled it again and finally Rivera clinched it 4-3 for Italy.

Italy were now faced with Brazil – comfortable 3-1 conquerors of Uruguay – in the Final and Pelé opened the scoring. Italy levelled, but then Brazil cut loose in the second half after Gérson scored in the 66th minute. Pelé laid the ball on for Jairzinho to sweep home the third before Carlos Alberto finished it off with a thundering shot. Brazil were worthy champions, the Jules Rimet trophy was theirs to keep and Mexico '70 had been a World Cup to savour in the memory.

I F IN THE 1950s HUNGARY were saddled with the title 'the best team never to have won the World Cup', then the 1970s marked a decade when that crown was passed on – to Holland.

This was the age of Total Football, a Dutch invention that did away with players sticking to a rigid format and instead allowed them to rotate. If a defender moved into attack, an attacker would move back to defend. It was a system that required complete concentration, swift thought, but above all, men who could play football, men comfortable on the ball.

The Dutch were lucky. On that front they had a very special team – Johan Cruyff and Johan Neeskens were just two stars in a team of real players. As their coach Rinus Michels said: 'You need at least seven world-class players to use the system; one less and you are in trouble.'

At the outset there had been 98 teams bidding to make the finals in West Germany, and England had fallen by the wayside, eliminated in the qualifying stages by Poland. The East European side were to be a force in the competition, coming through their Group Four matches with three wins out of three, including victories over Italy and Argentina, and a tally of 12 goals scored against three conceded.

In Group Three Holland were frighteningly good, strolling past Uruguay 2-0, held by a battling Sweden to 0-0 and then destroying Bulgaria 4-1. Meanwhile in Group Two Scotland – the lone British representatives – were to be punished for a lack of goals against Zaire. The group boiled down to who could score the most against the African side. Scotland won 2-0, Brazil 3-0 and Yugoslavia 9-0. Yugoslavia and Brazil progressed and Scotland were in familiar territory, the airport lounge looking for an early plane home.

Group One was all about Germany, both East and West qualifying, East having the better of the game between the two countries and winning 1-0. So on to stage two.

A new round of group matches had Holland, Brazil, East Germany and Argentina in section A while section B had West Germany, Poland, Sweden and Yugoslavia. By this stage the teams were well into their stride and the Dutch were getting better and better.

Argentina were crushed 4-0, East Germany 2-0 and Brazil also 2-0. Brazil, now without Pelé and running on a tank of memories, scored one superb goal against East Germany when Rivelino struck a wickedly swerving free-kick in their 1-0 win. That apart, they were second best to the Dutch.

Group B was a much closer affair, with West Germany far from confident in beating Yugoslavia 2-0 and Sweden 4-2. This left them in a head to head with Poland who had beaten Sweden 1-0 and Yugoslavia 2-1. It was a winner-takes-all contest played on a waterlogged pitch that favoured the more muscular

Germans. There was drama along the way with Jan Tomaszewski saving a penalty, but helpless when a deflected shot ran into the path of Gerd Müller, who scored the only goal of the game. Poland went on to take third place after a play-off with Brazil, but all eyes were on the Final in Munich and what should have been the crowning moment for Dutch football.

Indeed, the way the game started it looked as though Holland would take it at a canter. The kick-off was Holland's and they played the ball forward with a series of neat passes, not a German player getting near the ball. As Cruyff strode into the penalty area, he was brought down by Hoeness. Penalty – and Neeskens scored, 1-0 to Holland, only two minutes gone and a German yet to kick the ball.

Holland's technical supremacy bordered on the arrogant, but Germany were not going to give up without a fight and were level when they won a penalty and Breitner scored. Two minutes before half-time Gerd Müller put them ahead when he controlled

a less-than-perfect cross from Bonhof, dragged the ball back and fired home a shot past Jan Jongbloed. It was Müller's 68th and final goal for his country – and the most important of the lot.

The second half belonged totally to Holland, but Sepp Maier in the German goal would not be beaten and when he foiled Neeskens with one stunning save, the Dutch seemed to realize that this was not going to be their day. In the end pragmatic football had won out but Holland had given the game a new direction.

A look at the tournament's leading goalscorers is proof that their talk of Total Football was not hot air. They scored 15 goals during the competition, of which Neeskens hit five and Johnny Rep four, the rest shared between a team of players willing to take on the responsibility themselves.

Holland were to reach the Final again in 1978 in Argentina, where they lost 3-1 to the hosts in extra-time. They were still playing Total Football, but perhaps did not quite have the required number of world-class players to carry it off convincingly. For all that it was a joy to watch and although they won nothing, they certainly brought some footballing sunshine to the 1970s.

1990

Bigger is not always better, as Italia '90 proved. There were 112 sides bidding to make the finals – and there were 24 teams involved in those final stages. Yet such was the value of the prize that the negative rather than the positive came to the fore. This was a World Cup that suffered an acute shortage of goals – a meagre 115 in 52 games. Worse, there were 164 bookings and 16 sendings-off. The stars to illuminate the stage never made it out of the wings.

But for all that there were great moments and heartening ones. None more so than the England revival – a fabulous run that took them to the semi-final and, but for a penalty shoot-out failure, would have led to the Final and surely victory over a desperately poor Argentina.

The competition started in sensational style when Cameroon kicked-off against defending champions Argentina, ignored the script when Omam Biyik put them ahead and then had the nerve to hold on for victory. African football had arrived.

Argentina were to squeeze through to the last 16 by the skin of their teeth; Cameroon, despite a Group B 4-0 drubbing by the already eliminated

USSR, went forward more confidently. In Group A Italy, with three wins out of three and a new hero in Toto Schillaci, advanced easily enough with Czechoslovakia. Brazil had no problems in Group C but did not really appear to be firing, Group D belonged to Germany and Group E to Spain.

England were in Group F with Holland, the Republic of Ireland and Egypt. There were six matches played and only one positive result, England beating Egypt 1-0 while drawing 1-1 with Ireland and 0-0 with Holland.

The last 16 followed a knockout format and Cameroon kept marching on, beating Colombia 2-1 in extra-time. Czechoslovakia thumped Costa Rica 4-1 while Brazil succumbed 1-0 to Argentina. The match of the round was between West Germany and Holland. A fiery encounter, which saw Germany's Rudi Völler and Holland's Frank Rijkaard sent off after a spitting and then push-and-shove incident, was settled 2-1 in Germany's favour.

The Republic of Ireland's terrific run continued, thanks to a penalty shoot-out success over Romania, winning 5-4 after a 0-0 draw, while Italy were 2-0 winners over Uruguay. Spain lost 2-1 to Yugoslavia in extra-time and England beat Belgium with the last kick of extra-time. Penalties were looming when a free-kick was hoisted into the heart of the Belgian defence. England's David Platt swivelled and volleyed home for a goal that broke Belgian hearts.

In the quarter-finals Argentina revealed their true colours, coming through against Yugoslavia on penalties after a 0-0 draw. Ireland lost 1-0 to Italy – but were to beat them memorably by the same margin in New York four years later – while Germany were 1-0 conquerors of Czechoslovakia. England were made to battle on against Cameroon.

The African nation went behind to a David Platt goal, levelled through a penalty 16 minutes into the second half and then went ahead four minutes later. England seemed incapable of breaching the

Africans' stout defence, but a trip on Gary Lineker gave England a chink of light that was looking increasingly unlikely. Extra-time, Lineker was fouled in the box again and England were through to their first World Cup semi-final on foreign soil.

Both matches were tight. Italy and Argentina drew 1-1 and went to penalties where Argentina won and a host nation sobbed. England also drew 1-1 with Germany and again it was penalties. Chris Waddle and Stuart Pearce were denied and Germany were on their way to a third World Cup triumph. Memories of what might have been, of Gascoigne's tears, of Lineker's goals, still haunt every England fan.

The Final was a drab affair ruined by Argentina's intentions to go for the draw and the lottery of the penalty shoot-out. Instead it was a penalty late in the game which settled it. Völler went down in the box, Brehme calmly converted the kick and that was it. Two Argentines were sent off and a world rejoiced that the South Americans – true pantomime villains in Italy – had not made off with football's crown jewel, the World Cup.

Golden Moments, Golden Days, Golden Players

THERE CAN BE NO GREATER footballing high, no greater footballing low. The game is over, the World Cup has been lost and won. The trophy, bedecked in the coloured ribbons of the winning nation, glints before the eye, while all around a wall of noise invades the head. The moment has come, the winning captain steps forward, exhausted but running on the adrenaline of the moment, the hand trembles. A handshake and the trophy is handed over, lifted in triumph as the stadium noise builds even higher. It is the sort of moment you want to last forever.

For the losers the drama is witnessed in stunned disbelief, the cheers and shouts of the crowd a dull, buzzing irritant, a tinnitus hum like a painful hangover. The mind plays all sorts of tricks, posing question after question: 'Why isn't it us?' ... 'What if that shot had gone in instead of hitting the post?' ... 'Have I let my country down?'

The exhaustion is complete, the legs want to buckle but the rites of passage must be completed before the sanctuary of the dressing room and the door can be slammed shut on the chaos brought about by defeat. For the losing captain the weight of the world on the shoulders is crushing. In such moments perspectives become blurred. Reaching a World Cup Final is a mighty achievement, a source of pride. A golden moment.

So rare an honour is winning a World Cup that only six countries and 15 men have stepped forward to accept that famous trophy. It is perhaps the ultimate football list, some captains' table: Jose Nasazzi of Uruguay was the first; Combi of Italy in 1934; Meazza also of Italy in 1938; Varela when Uruguay beat Brazil in Rio de Janeiro in 1950; Walter of West Germany in 1954; Bellini of Brazil in Sweden in 1958; Gylmar the Brazilian goalkeeper in 1962; Bobby Moore at Wembley for England in 1966; Carlos Alberto, the immaculate Brazilian defender who stood solid in Mexico in 1970. Next it was the turn of the German midfield general, Franz Beckenbauer. In 1978 another defender, Passarella of Argentina, took his turn; Dino Zoff in 1982 for Italy; Maradona was the Argentine captain in 1986; Lothar Matthaus collected it for Germany in Italy in 1990; while Dunga of Brazil was the last man to receive the prize, in the USA in 1994.

That roll call includes three goalkeepers, but astonishingly only once has a World Cup captain scored in the Final. How ironic too that it should be a defender. The man – Carlos Alberto of Brazil. The place and year – Mexico 1970. It was certainly a special World Cup, with the quality of football sublime, the matches throughout filled with

drama. There was the classic England v Brazil group game, the epic West Germany against England quarter-final. Then in extra-time in their quarter-final, Italy exploded into life against Mexico, coming through to win 4-1.

In the semi-finals the Italians were involved in another extra-time thriller when beating Germany 4-3 in a ding-dong battle. Then the Final, the artistry of Brazil being given a full canvas as they won 4-1. As for Carlos Alberto's goal – it was worth the wait. Brazil were 3-1 ahead and four minutes remained. Jairzinho found Pelé with a perfectly weighted through-pass; he controlled it as only Pelé could and, aware of every-thing that was happening around him, laid the ball off for his captain to crash home a powerful shot.

No captain, as the list proves, has ever lifted the trophy twice although Maradona was skipper of Argentina when they won in 1986 and lost in 1990, while the German Karl-Heinz Rummenigge was twice the skipper of losing finalists.

THE PLAYER OF 1970 was Jairzinho. Born on Christmas Day 1944 in Caxias, a suburb of Rio de Janeiro, Jairzinho signed as an amateur for Botafogo in 1961 and became a professional shortly after winning a gold medal in the 1963 Pan American Games. Capped by Brazil in 1964, he came to England for the 1966 World Cup but made just three appear-ances, undone by a fiery temper, injuries and defenders who buttoned him up tight.

By 1970, however, he had established himself in the Brazilian side and this time the best of the world's defenders could not cope with his electric pace, his long-striding running and sublime ball-control.

There were goals against Czechoslovakia, England, Romania, Peru, Uruguay and then Italy in the Final. He was the first man to score in every round of the finals and in total was to play 87 times for Brazil scoring 37 goals, coming back from a broken leg in

1971 to play in the 1974 World Cup. Jairzinho had a brief spell in France with Olympique Marseille, but otherwise was loyal to Botafogo.

Jairzinho was the right man for a perfectly balanced Brazilian side yet amazingly was not the top scorer in the 1970 competition. That honour went to West Germany's Gerd Müller.

THERE ARE goalscoring heroes and goalscoring legends. Geoff Hurst of England belongs in the latter category because of one remarkable afternoon in late July 1966 – the day England won the World Cup. Hurst was the only man to score a hat-trick in a World Cup Final and became a household name overnight. But as the build-up to the World Cup of that year began, Hurst was simply a member of the squad and had played just five matches for England, scoring only once.

Born on 8 December 1941 in Ashton-under-Lyme in Lancashire, he signed as a professional with West Ham in 1959, but played just eight matches in two seasons. The transformation came when Ron Greenwood, the West Ham manager later to become the England boss, moved Hurst into attack. It worked a treat as West Ham won the FA Cup in 1964 and the European Cup Winners' Cup the next season.

Sir Alf Ramsey's first choice for England was Jimmy Greaves, but after a stuttering start – a 0-0 draw with Uruguay and 2-0 wins over France and Mexico – and an an injury to Greaves, Ramsey made some changes and brought in Hurst.

He scored the only goal of the quarter-final against Argentina, was in the side that beat Portugal 2-1 in the semi-final and was winning his eighth cap in the World Cup Final. The first goal came in the 18th minute when he headed in a quickly taken free-kick by Bobby Moore. It was 2-2 at full-time with Martin Peters scoring the other England goal, and then extra-time.

Hurst's second goal is perhaps the most controversial in the history of football. Alan Ball raced past Karl-Heinz Schnellinger and crossed the ball to Hurst, who was positioned with his back to goal. He turned and shot, the ball flying upwards, striking the bar and coming down. Roger Hunt, following up, wheeled away to celebrate the goal as the West Germans protested that the ball had not crossed the line.

The referee consulted the linesman and the goal was given. England led 3-2. Even today, detailed examination of the film of that goal is inconclusive – but in cases like this the referee's decision is always final!

In the closing minutes the Germans poured forward in numbers, but when Bobby Moore broke up another attack, he did not hoof it into the stands, instead he looked up, saw Hurst and sent his club and country team-mate galloping forward to smash home England's fourth and his third of the match.

Hurst went on to play 49 times for England and score 24 goals, but no moment was ever going to match that golden afternoon.

FERENC PUSKÁS was one great player not fully rewarded by the World Cup. One of the greatest forwards of any era, he played 84 times for Hungary and scored 83 goals. He was a key member of the Hungary side that lost only one match between 1951 and 1956 – the tragedy being that the one match was the World Cup Final of 1954.

During the early 1950s Hungary – affection-ately known as the Mighty Magyars – were the best team in the world. Puskás won his first cap as an 18-year-old in 1945 and went on to win an Olympic gold medal in 1952.

A member of the Honved team, he was on tour in South America with his club in 1956 when the Hungarian uprising broke out. Along with team-mates Kocsis and Czibor, he decided not to return home, went to Vienna and, 12 months later, joined Real Madrid.

The Spanish side was one of the all-time great club sides and Puskás was to score 35 goals in 39 European Cup matches, including four in the 1960 7-3 win over Eintracht Frankfurt in Glasgow – it was the club's fifth consecutive European Cup triumph. He retired in 1966, having finished his international career playing four times for his adopted country, Spain.

PELÉ – the name means football, the name means goals. The legend of the man spans four World Cups, but is synonymous with all World Cup football. He has two winner's medals and played a total of 1,363 matches for clubs and country, scoring 1,281 goals.

Born in October 1940 in Tres Coracoes in Brazil, Pelé was a first-team regular with Santos by the time he was 16, and in 1957 scored on his inter-national debut.

He was in the Brazilian side that went to Sweden for the 1958 World Cup, scored a hat-trick in the semi-final against France and another two in the Final win over Sweden. This was the first televised World Cup and the world was ready for a star like Pelé.

His agility and athleticism were complemented by magical ball skills, a wicked shot, superb heading ability and the knack of reading a game while at the heart of the action. His first goal in the Final summed him up perfectly. The match was in the 56th minute and Brazil led 2-1. He was in the middle of the penal-ty area with his back to goal when the ball was deliv-ered to him, chest high. He trapped it, lobbed it over his head and then, in the same swift movement, spun

round the defender to volley home the ball. It broke Sweden's heart and their resistance crumbled.

Most players could live the life of Riley off such a moment. Not Pelé. This was the sort of magic he produced game after game and although he had a miserable World Cup in Chile in 1962 and in England in 1966, he was the elder statesman of a brilliant new Brazil in 1970.

The World Cup was won again, this time for keeps. Pelé scored the opening goal in the Final and the man of legend had proved once again he was every bit as good as the golden deeds ascribed to him.

THERE SEEMS TO BE A PLAYER for every era and in the 1970s it was the Dutchman Johan Cruyff, like Puskás destined never to possess a winner's medal – yet for all that, he was an enormous influence on his country and on world football.

Cruyff became the first £1 million player in 1973 when he left Ajax for Barcelona, and he was the captain of the exceptional Holland side that reached the 1974 World Cup Final.

Born on 25 April 1947 within walking dis-

tance of the Ajax ground in Amsterdam, he first played for them in 1964. In nine years he was to be instrumental in them winning six Dutch championships, four cups and three European Cups. He made his Holland debut in 1966.

Eight years later, having been voted European Footballer of the Year in 1971, he was the pivot for the Dutch revolution, the concept of Total Football. It was a sensational side, as thrilling and dynamic as the Mighty Magyars had been in the early 1950s.

Neeskens, Rep, Krol, Rensenbrink and Haan were all superb footballers in their own right. With Cruyff prompting them, they were great. Holland waltzed through the 1974 competition, trotting through the first round of group matches and then accelerating in the second phase – a super group.

Argentina were beaten 4-0, East Germany 2-0 and then the defending champions, Brazil, were crushed 2-0. Holland looked unstoppable, especially as West Germany's progress had been far less assured.

In the Final, Cruyff produced a moment that encapsulated all his ability. The Dutch had the kick-off, the ball came to Cruyff and he advanced up field, found himself in the German penalty area and was fouled. Penalty to Holland, the Germans yet to touch the ball and less than a minute gone. It was as if Cruyff and ball were one. In the end it proved too good a start for Holland, who settled back against a German side that would not give up. They were technically inferior, but had the engine to keep on going when faced with a mountain to climb – and perseverance paid off as they won 2-1.

In 1950 the Brazilians were so confident of winning that they had a victory song written before the Final – which they then lost 2-1 to Uruguay. Then four years later the Hungarians lost when overwhelming favourites to win against the Germans. Holland fell into the same category – ultimately, too good for their own good.

MEMORIES OF MARADONA are soured by the mind's replay of the 'Hand of God' goal. There was the diminutive but stocky Argentine charging into the England penalty box, leaping next to Peter Shilton and fisting the ball into the goal. Everyone bar the referee saw the villain's hand at work, so the goal stood. It put Argentina 1-0 up and four minutes later Maradona displayed the brilliant side of his Jekyll and Hyde character.

This time the goal was 100 per cent legitimate. Out wide right and in his own half, he picked up the ball and moved forward. He went round Peter Beardsley, Peter Reid, Gary Stevens, Terry Butcher and then Terry Fenwick before sliding the ball past Shilton.

The England players were completely baffled by the man's movement and ball-control and it was one of the best individual goals seen in a World Cup. Argentina went on to win the 1986 tournament.

Maradona played for Argentinos Juniors from 1975 to 1982 before moving to Europe, appearing for Barcelona in Spain and then Napoli – but he was a man unable to cope with fame. Heavy drinking, women and drug abuse culminated in his arrest for possession of cocaine in 1991. Banned from playing for 15 months, his best days were gone – but in his prime Maradona had been compared with Pelé and his ball-control, powerful shooting and ability to beat a man were second to none.

Mario Zagallo was the first man to play for and then manage a World Cup winning side. He was in the Brazil team that won the trophy in 1958 and 1962, and was at the helm when Brazil won in 1970 in Mexico.

Franz Beckenbauer became the first man to captain and manage a World Cup winning side. The West German midfielder has been one of their most influential figures in the game, both as player and manager. A skilled grafter, he was credited with inventing the role of the attacking sweeper and indeed it was his calm on the field that helped Germany to success in the 1974 Final against Holland.

Beckenbauer was born on 11 September 1945 and played most of his club football with Bayern Munich, figuring in three World Cups. He was a loser in 1966, a semi-finalist in 1970 and eventually triumphed four years later. At club level, Bayern Munich were heading towards three European Cups between 1974 and 1976.

In 1977 he moved to America and New York Cosmos, then had a short spell at Hamburg before retiring. He was appointed manager of West Germany in 1984. Two years later he led his country to the Final of the World Cup against Argentina; then in 1990 took his revenge as Germany beat the same opposition 1-0. Beckenbauer, as player and manager, had proved himself to be the best.

ABEL LAFLEUR'S place in World Cup history is assured. He was the man commissioned to create the original Jules Rimet trophy, won outright by Brazil in 1970 after they beat Italy 4-1 in Mexico.

Lafleur's 30cm creation weighed 4 kg and its official title was 'Victoire aux ailes d'or'. But it was not just the object of ultimate desire for the world's football teams – it was also coveted by thieves.

The trophy went missing four months before the 1966 World Cup finals were due to begin. Insured for £30,000, it had been on display at a stamp exhibition at Central Hall in Westminster, London when it was stolen. The thief ignored the stamps worth millions and disappeared with the trophy. A few days later a ransom demand for £15,000 was made – it proved to be a hoax – and the FA were facing severe embarrassment for losing the game's greatest treasure.

A week after the theft, David Corbett took his dog, Pickles, for a walk in Norwood, South London. The black and white mongrel disappeared into a hedge and started digging furiously, unearthing a parcel and the lost trophy. Corbett collected a £6,000 reward and Pickles went to the celebration banquet to lick the plates clean.

The second time the trophy went missing there was no Pickles around to save the day. Brazil had it on display in the Brazilian Football Confederation offices until 19 December 1983, when it vanished into thin air.

Two men were arrested, but the Jules Rimet trophy was gone, melted down for its gold value. Brazil, however, were presented with a £25,000 replica in 1984.

A TOUCH OF GENIUS and a split second is all it takes to make for a golden World Cup moment. Remarkable saves, like Gordon Banks diving from one post to the other to deny Pelé and Brazil in 1970; Carlos Valderrama, the red-headed Afro king of Colombia causing havoc in the USA in 1994; Hristo Stoitchkov and Iordan Letchkov striking late for Bulgaria to beat Germany in the same tournament; Roberto Baggio of Italy turning the tables on Bulgaria in their 1994 semi-final.

Going back to 1990, Omam Biyik scoring for Cameroon as they kicked-off the tournament in Italy against champions Argentina and won 1-0. From the same camp there was the mercurial Roger Milla, a man so old that he refused to give his age, and generous estimates put him at 38. Milla was a revelation and his goalscoring celebrations a sight to behold as he tangoed with the corner flag. There were tears from Paul Gascoigne of England and joy for Germany as they won yet another penalty shoot-out; a system to decide games that is yet to go against the Germans.

Spain 1982 belonged to Italy and Paolo Rossi, a man returning to the world stage having been banned for two years after match-fixing allegations. In the same tournament, the German goalkeeper Harald Schumacher poleaxed France's Battiston when he was through on goal and, remarkably, was allowed to stay on the pitch. This was the gifted French side of Platini, Tigana and Giresse, the team that went on to win the 1984 European Championship. The Germans won the semi-final on penalties after a thrilling 3-3 draw.

For every show-stealing moment and star turn, there have been supporting players putting in performances to make it all happen. Cruyff in the Holland side of 1974 was surrounded by players who could have hogged the limelight for themselves had he not been around – Rep, Neeskens, Rensenbrink. England in 1966 had the peerless Bobby Moore and the battling Nobby Stiles; Brazil in the 1950s and 60s had Garrincha; the USSR had Lev Yashin in goal – all players subscribing to the ethos that the total of the team can, with hard work and the right attitude, be greater than the sum of its 11 parts.

There have been extraordinary feats that have been impossible to repeat. In 1934 Raimundo Orsi scored the first of Italy's two goals in the 2-1 Final defeat of Czechoslovakia with a sensational piece of play. Orsi weaved through the Czech defence, had the goal in his sights and while feinting to the left, shot with his right foot and scored. Asked to repeat the incredible double-footed feat the following day for waiting cameramen, Orsi had 20 goes and failed every time.

I N THE BEGINNING there were 13 teams and only two of them were founder members of FIFA – France and Belgium. By the 1994 World Cup in America 144 teams dreamed of playing in the finals of the World Cup and 24 made it.

For France '98 the number has grown again – and so too have the finalists. There will be 32 countries playing before the biggest TV audience ever, and a live crowd that has swelled dramatically tournament on tournament.

The number of spectators in Chile in 1962 was 896,336. The figure had climbed to 2,517,348 in Italia '90 and then 3,587,538 in the USA. The expanded format of the finals in France will see live attendances shoot up again.

L UIS MONTI played for Argentina in the 1930 World Cup Final and then for Italy four years later; while Jose Altafini was with Brazil in 1958 and Italy in 1962. Puskás had a World Cup with Hungary in 1954 and Spain in 1962, after moving there to play his club football, while Jose Santamaria was a Uruguay player in 1954 and also played for Spain in 1962.

T HE FASTEST GOAL in the history of the World Cup was scored in Chile in 1962 by the Czech player Vaclav Masek. He was on target within 15 seconds of the start of the match against Mexico although Czechoslovakia lost the match 3-1. Despite this they recovered and went on to reach the Final where they were beaten 3-1 by Brazil.

FOR MANY PLAYERS appearing in a World Cup campaign is a career-high, the stuff of dreams, and few go on to win the main prize. Yet the contribution of Leslaw Cmikiewicz of Poland to his side's 1974 campaign, which saw them march to a 3rd-place Final with Brazil – they won 1-0 – takes some beating.

During the tournament he played six times for Poland in seven matches, yet was involved in only 102 minutes of football and his longest stint on the field was 33 minutes in a 2-1 win over Yugoslavia.

The beauty of the World Cup is that it brings the best of football together for a month; a time for indulging in the brilliance and breathtaking skills of some of the world's leading players. You cannot guarantee the quality of individual matches, but in France '98 you can be certain that there will be many more rich moments added to the treasured memories banked from the other 15 tournaments played since 1930.

The quality of the cast promises that much – Brazil with Ronaldo, Romário and Roberto Carlos are able to destroy any side, with Ronaldo heralded as the pre-tournament star of France '98. The Italians have Christian Vieri, Alessandro del Piero and Paolo Maldini.

Yet it is the smaller countries that throw up the real stars, the players to make a name for themselves and then become leading lights in European club football. Look out for the already much-rated Chilean Marcelo Salas; Spain have the talented Raul, Nigeria Jay Okacha.

England's confident youngsters, David Beckham, Paul Scholes and Nicky Butt can shine before an appreciative audience, while Alan Shearer has the chance to become the first Englishman since Gary Lineker, in Mexico 1986, to win the Golden Boot for being the leading scorer.

The stage is set, the cast ready to perform.

The Captains' Table

I T IS SAID THAT FOOTBALL is a game where the role of the captain is peripheral. He puts on an armband, walks to the centre circle, shakes hands with his opposite number and the referee, calls heads or tails and then makes the taxing decision, kick-off or ends.

It can be like that – but then look at the successful teams in football history and you will find they all have captains who inspire, men who lead by example and bring out the best not only from the rest of the side but also the squad and the club. They are the figureheads, the focal point for all that energy on the pitch, the men upon whose shoulders the weight of expectancy sits. Certainly in cricket and rugby, the captain makes crucial decisions that can wildly swing the fortunes of his team. In football the effect of the skipper is less obvious but potentially as dramatic.

Would the successful England side of the 1960s have been the same without Bobby Moore to lead them? How about the Germany led by Franz Beckenbauer? Pelé did not lift the World Cup as skipper but although Maradona did, he would hardly qualify as a footballing role model.

What of England and their 36 captains since 1945? The list is an impressive catalogue of leading lights in the game, but many players have done the job for a match or two and then fallen back among the rest of the foot soldiers. Only seven players have led their country more than 20 times. Those seven are Billy Wright, who did it 91 times, Johnny Haynes 22, Emlyn Hughes 23, Kevin Keegan 31, Bryan Robson 63, Gary Lineker 20 and the England captain of captains – Bobby Moore with 92 matches as skipper.

BOBBY MOORE

T HE ART OF GOOD CAPTAINCY is thinking ahead; taking into account the probable turn of events and preparing for all eventualities. It is also about setting a good example – and in this respect Bobby Moore was the best of the lot.

When England won the World Cup on that emotional July day in 1966, when Wembley stadium was buzzing, when his team-mates were drunk on the euphoria of their success, Bobby Moore remembered his good manners. He climbed the 39 steps to the Royal Box and edged down the passage towards the Queen, who was to present him with the Jules Rimet trophy. Suddenly Moore stopped and wiped his hands on the velvet drapes of the box. He didn't want to dirty the Queen's white gloves.

Bobby Moore was born on 12 April 1941 in Barking. He signed for West Ham as a professional in 1958, making his debut against Manchester United. He would go on to play 642 times for the club and win an FA Cup and a European Cup Winners' Cup. Despite his quiet demeanour, Moore was a fiercely ambitious man, ready to listen and act on the advice of people he respected.

He knew his only flaw was a lack of raw pace, but rather than let that get him down, he more than compensated for this weakness by becoming one of the most complete readers of the game. Moore knew when and where the opposition were going to play the ball, he knew where their strikers were going to run almost before they did and he was able to counter any threat.

Alf Ramsey saw early that Moore had what it took to be a leader of men and appointed him as skipper in his 12th international. That left Ramsey free to shape the team he wanted, knowing that Moore would hold it all together – and that is precisely what happened.

Unflappable, Moore saw his role as more than just a stopper; from defence, attack could be created. Witness that fourth goal in the 1966 World Cup. The whole of the England team were begging Moore to thump the ball into the stands. Instead, playing by his instinct, he looked for Hurst and set up the goal that put England's supremacy beyond any doubt. When Moore tackled, he did it with the express aim of coming away with the ball. And from there he could construct for the benefit of his team.

Always dignified, he came through the stress of being accused of stealing a bracelet in Bogota, Colombia before the Mexico World Cup and put under house arrest. It later transpired that the owners of the shop had accused other celebrities of theft, forcing them to pay up to avoid damaging headlines. The case against Moore collapsed and two years later the shop owners were charged with conspiracy.

In 1970 Moore played his finest game in the group match against Brazil. Moore and Pelé were head to head and although England lost 1-0, Moore came out of the encounter more revered than ever. The respect between the two was evident as they swapped shirts at the end of the game. When Moore died of cancer on 24 February 1993, Pelé said: 'Words cannot sum up the great grief I feel for my great friend. He was one of the world's finest defenders and a great sportsman.'

Moore finished his playing career in Fulham, appeared in American soccer then returned home for an unsuccessful spell managing Southend. When he died he left behind a contribution to English football that is hard to express with words. He was instrumental in England's finest footballing hours; he was one of the most complete defenders the game has ever seen; he was a gentleman and an example to all who came across him. Proof of his greatness can be found in the number of rivals, home and abroad – including Pelé and Franz Beckenbauer – who could admire him for his skills and genuinely call him a friend.

ENGLAND AFTER MOORE

CAPTAINS came and captains went after Moore, with only Emlyn Hughes of Liverpool having anything like an extended run. Hughes' 23-match reign came at a time when England were struggling just to qualify for major competitions – thinking about winning them was another matter entirely.

The men asked to fill Moore's boots were all good footballers; no one would quibble at having Alan Ball (6), Gerry Francis (1), Mick Channon (2), Mick Mills (8), Phil Thompson (6), Trevor Cherry (1), Dave Watson (1) or Ray Wilkins (1) in the side, but none could give England the lead and direction that was needed.

Next came Kevin Keegan – an inspirational player whether he was up front or in the midfield – but still the slump in English football continued. He was leading the side as it failed to reach the 1978 World Cup in Argentina, pipped by Italy on goal difference. While Keegan had the skill – and the fearlessness – to turn a match by himself, he was more the dashing, daring cavalier type than a natural leader of men.

It was back to the drawing board for England, with Spain 1982 the next target, and again Keegan was the man leading the country in four of the eight qualifying games. He was skipper for a trip to Switzerland that ended in a 2-1 defeat; scored one in the 3-1 victory over Hungary in Budapest; led the side in a 2-1 defeat by Norway but redeemed that as Hungary were beaten 1-0 at Wembley.

By this stage Keegan, now at Southampton having enjoyed his best days first with Liverpool and then in Germany at SV Hamburg, was nearing the end of his playing career. In fact his last international was in Spain, when he replaced Tony Woodcock against the host nation in the second round of the tournament. Two goalless draws ended England's interest in the competition.

Keegan then joined Newcastle to finish his playing days and went into retirement in 1984 before re-emerging in 1992 to manage the club, leading them from the brink of relegation to the Second Division into the Premiership. Then in January 1997, Keegan suddenly resigned before later reappearing at Fulham.

BRYAN ROBSON

They called him Captain Marvel, and he certainly was. Bryan Robson was the sort of captain players would follow into the fires of hell without giving it a second thought. He led by example and stuck to the maxim that he would not expect anyone to do something he would not do himself. And there wasn't much he wouldn't do.

He won a total of 90 caps and was captain 63 times, figures that would have been higher had Robson not been as courageous as he was. The abiding memory is of Robson in the 1986 World Cup in Mexico. In the preceding season he had dislocated his shoulder, and his place in the final England party that flew out for the World Cup in June looked very much in doubt. In fact, had it been anyone other than Robson trying to come back from injury, they would not have made the flight.

Bobby Robson, the England manager at the time, decided to gamble. Robson was worth his weight in gold as a player, and as a presence in the squad his value was double that. Sadly for England, it was a risk that didn't pay off.

Robson was substituted in the opening game, a 1-0 defeat by Portugal, but came back for the second match with Morocco. In the first half, his shoulder went again and there was no way back for him this time. In the face of adversity, however, England soldiered on. The midfield was reshaped, with Peter Reid, Trevor Steven and Steve Hodge left to do the spade-

work and suddenly England were up and flying. They beat Poland 3-0, then Paraguay 3-0 in the last 16 before falling 2-1 to Argentina in the quarter-final.

Robson flew home for an operation, medical opinion certain that the job should be done properly this time. Amazingly, by the middle of October 1986 he was back playing for his country. And if Robson played, then Robson led. England reached the Italia '90 World Cup, where he was injured again, but by that stage his international career had certainly reached its peak and the England midfield was now the territory of younger guns, men like David Platt and Paul Gascoigne. Robson eventually moved into management with Middlesbrough. He played on for England until 1992, making his last appearance in a 1-0 home win over Turkey.

There is no doubt that Robson would be in an all-time England squad – and had it not been for Bobby Moore, he would have been head and shoulders above the rest of the candidates in the race to captain it. There can be no greater compliment than that.

LIFE AFTER THE ROBSONS

DAVID PLATT, the man who effectively replaced Bryan Robson in the England midfield, was to lead his country 19 times. Like Robson, Platt was an explosive midfield player who

made a habit of coming late into the penalty area to score crucial goals.

Articulate and intelligent, Platt was more of a ghost player, appearing here and there, suddenly looming up on opponents. He was not a Robson-type, the man for the hand-to-hand combat of the midfield. While his goals inspired and lifted the side and he could stoke the fires within himself admirably, he was never the sort of player his team-mates would look to for a lead – simply because that was not his style.

Platt moved from Aston Villa to Bari in Italy for £5.5 million, from Bari to Juventus for £6.5 million, from Juventus to Sampdoria for £5.2 million. He then returned to England and Arsenal for £4.75 million, but by this stage his best international days were gone.

Another player to have a decent run as captain was Gary Lineker – the former Leicester, Everton, Barcelona and Tottenham striker. If ever there was the ideal model for what a captain should be, then Lineker was it. Here was a man who, throughout a long and distinguished club career and 80 England matches, was never once sent off, nor even booked. One of the very best strikers to have come out of the English game, Lineker was lethal inside a penalty area, his speed electric, his instincts razor sharp. On top of that he was brave. He was to score 48 goals for his country and could have equalled Bobby Charlton's record of 49 goals had he not missed a penalty against Brazil.

Lineker announced that he was going to retire after England had played in the 1992 European Championship in Sweden. Three matches later it was all over – England were out having drawn two and lost one game. Lineker had not scored, and 29 minutes from the end of the game with Sweden he suffered the indignity of being substituted by Graham Taylor. Lineker's world had ended with a whimper.

What of Lineker as captain? The playing record undoubtedly stands up under the harshest spotlight; the disciplinary record saintly. Off the field he was the model of politeness and consideration – but as a captain, he played in the wrong place. Strikers are

lone wolves, predatory beasts. They don't drag flagging team-mates into the game, they don't, as a rule, dig in when the going gets rough. They prowl and they glare. Even Lineker could cast a withering look in the direction of a team-mate who had not played him the ball when perfectly placed, or had come up with a clumsy pass. Captaincy for forwards, in most instances, is a burden that blunts the cutting edge.

Stuart Pearce has the Bryan Robson fight, but although he has led his country with pride and fire, he came to the job in his twilight years. Tony Adams has done a superb job at Arsenal. As a defender he can see what is going on around him and he has proved himself a leader, cajoling and encouraging his Arsenal defence to hold firm, coming into attack when needed and scoring vital goals. Adams may have had his problems off the pitch, but today he is a different man, older – but not too old – and wiser. He is an example to his peers and they respect him. Yet Adams has been plagued by injury and he is not Glenn

Hoddle's first choice. Nor is Paul Ince, the first black player to skipper a full England side. Ince has the fire of Robson – he played in the same Manchester United team for long enough – and he has the skill to inspire and a will to win that cannot be questioned. Yet the man most likely to lead the way in France is Alan Shearer.

Perhaps it is a sign of England's growing confidence that suddenly there are a number of strong candidates for the captaincy; men who in other eras would have walked into the job. Shearer is a forward who breaks the mould, proving that players in that position can make good skippers. Yet he is a different striker to Lineker. Shearer is the pillar of the England attack; a man who will hold the ball up and wait for support. His territory is not just the six-yard box, it is the penalty area and beyond. He looks to bring team-mates into the game, he will lay the ball off to them, run into the box and await the return. For a striker, Shearer is a very 'sociable' player.

Blessed with speed, a venomous shot and good physical strength, Shearer stands tall as a guiding light for England, respected by his team-mates and rated around the world. He was a success in Euro '96 and has an unquenchable thirst for goals. He drives a team by example, is diplomatic off the field and it is not difficult to see why he is the appointed man. Like Robson, he is fearless; he is the Harry Hotspur carrying England's hopes on the footballing battlefields of the world.

GOALKEEPERS AS CAPTAINS

FRANK SWIFT

ENGLAND have used four goalkeepers as captains in the post-War years – Frank Swift was the first-ever goalkeeping captain of the national side and led the team twice. The first time was against Italy in Turin in 1948. England won the match 4-0. Swift, who won 19 caps for England, was later killed in the Munich air disaster of 1958.

RAY CLEMENCE

THE LIVERPOOL and then Tottenham goalkeeper won 63 caps for England and led the side just once – against Brazil in 1981 at Wembley. England lost that night, 1-0.

PETER SHILTON

ENGLAND'S MOST CAPPED PLAYER – he won 125 – led his country 15 times, filling in as the experienced head in the camp when injuries robbed the side of the first-choice leader, although he did lead the side in seven out of eight games for a spell in 1983. Shilton closed his career in the play-off for third place in the Italia '90 World Cup, and to mark the occasion he was skipper for the day.

DAVID SEAMAN

When Shearer badly damaged his ankle in August 1997, England lost their skipper and, with a World Cup qualifying match coming up against Moldova, were in need of a substitute. David Seaman joined that short list of England skippers and had a successful night. Hardly bothered in goal, he was a virtual spectator as England won 4-0.

RIVAL CAPTAINS

FRANZ BECKENBAUER

The West German captain, and later coach, stands out as an exceptional leader. Confident in his skills, Beckenbauer was an inspirational figure who led by example. He skippered Germany to success in 1974 and coached them to two finals, winning the second, against Argentina in 1990. At club level he was an inspiration too as Bayern Munich won three successive European Cups.

Beckenbauer's place in the German team was assured from the time he made his debut in 1965 and after 103 caps, and an international career spanning 12 years, he retired from the world stage.

CARLOS ALBERTO

Another defender, and as a Brazilian therefore with a harder job than most, Carlos Alberto led the side to the World Cup in 1970. Rock solid in defence, it was left to him to hold together the strands of a supremely talented side. Individuals played for the team under his command and when the going was tough, he fired up his side and stopped them from collapsing – something South American teams have been more prone to than European sides.

He is the only World Cup winning captain to have scored in the Final. He scored eight goals in 58 international appearances between 1963 and 1977.

OBDULIO VARELA

It was always going to take an inspirational figure to lead a side to victory over Brazil in the World Cup on their own soil in 1950 – and Varela was that man for Uruguay. His side were 1-0 down in the Final, but the attacking centre-half, 33 at the time, was not giving up without a fight. His team came back and won 2-1.

Varela was back for the 1954 World Cup, but was injured in the 4-2 quarter-final win over England and retired from the game. He never played on a losing Uruguayan side in a World Cup.

GIUSEPPE MEAZZA

The Italian won two winner's medals, the first as one of the players in Italy in 1934, the second as captain of his country in 1938 in France. A forward, he scored twice on his international debut and hit 33 goals in 53 internationals – an Italian record that stood until beaten by Luigi Riva. He went on to coach the national side in 1962 and the San Siro stadium was renamed in his honour.

GROUP A

Brazil

(DEFENDING CHAMPIONS)

WORLD CUP RECORD

This is the country that sets the standards for all the others. Winners of three World Cups so that they got to keep the Jules Rimet trophy, they have since added the new trophy to the cabinet to claim four World Cup wins – more than any other nation. The names, down the years, still roll off the tongue – Pelé, Didi, Garrincha, Rivelino, Jairzinho, Zico and Socrates. The first World Cup was claimed in Sweden in 1958 where they won two of their three group matches – the blot was a 0-0 draw with England – then went on to knock out Wales 1-0 in the quarter-final. Then they really hit form, beating France 5-2 in the semi-final and hosts Sweden by the same margin in the Final. Amazingly, the Swedes went ahead but it was the magic of 17-year-old Pelé – he scored twice in the Final – that swung the contest. Four years later Brazil defended the trophy successfully – and without an injured Pelé. Spain and Mexico were beaten in the group stages then England were dispatched 3-1 in the quarter-finals. As in Sweden, Brazil saved their goalscoring spree for later in the tournament, beating hosts Chile 4-2 in the semi-final and Czechoslovakia 3-1 in the Final.

Disappointing in 1966, where they failed to progress past the group stage, Brazil were back on song in Mexico in 1970 with, Pelé apart, a side of new heroes. Jairzinho scored in every round as Brazil came through the group stage with three wins out of three;

crushed Peru 4-2 in the quarter-final; Uruguay 3-1 in the semi-final; and then demolished Italy 4-1. Pelé, putting the icing on a brilliant career, scored in the Final as Brazil made off with the cup for keeps. In 1974 they reached the second round, but a period of slump had set in. They qualified for every tournament onwards but it was not until America in 1994 that they really started to live up to their reputation. A last-16 win over the USA was followed by a thrilling quarter-final clash with Holland, Brazil winning 3-2. Sweden were beaten 1-0 in the semi-final and next up were Italy. The game, despite the stars on the field, was dire and drifted through extra-time at 0-0 with penalties to decide the issue. When Roberto Baggio missed with Italy's fifth and final penalty, Brazil were crowned World Champions. Today, with stars like Ronaldo and Bebeto, Brazil are a major and feared force.

MANAGER MARIO JORGE LOBO ZAGALLO

PROFILE

An old head, Mario Jorge Lobo Zagallo has been coaching national sides since 1970 when he was at the helm with Brazil for four years. He spent time with Kuwait, Saudi Arabia and the United Arab Emirates before picking up the reins with Brazil again in 1994. He was part of the backroom team to the 1994 winning side in the USA before moving into the hot-seat again. Zagallo, now 66, played with Rio de Janeiro sides América, Flamengo, Botafogo and won 37 caps and two World Cups.

KEY PLAYERS

ROBERTO CARLOS Age: 24 Club: Real Madrid (Spain)
► With over 40 caps, Roberto Carlos is a regular at international level and was an ever-present during Brazil's Copa América triumph in the summer of 1997.
► He is rated one of the best left-backs in the world, although he claims Paolo Maldini is still better: 'He's more experienced but I hope to overtake him soon.'

RONALDO Age: 21 Club: Inter Milan (Italy)
► Ronaldo is already being cited as Brazil's greatest talent since Pelé.
► At 16, he scored 54 goals in 54 matches in the Brazilian First Division and at 18, he scored 55 goals in 56 matches for PSV Eindhoven.
► Twice breaking the world record transfer fee, he moved to Barcelona and then for £18 million to Inter Milan in July 1997.

DENILSON Age: 20 Club: São Paulo
► Denilson is rumoured to be signing a £21.5 million deal with Spanish side Real Betis – which would make him the most expensive player in the world.
► A left-footed midfielder, he was a member of the Brazilian team that reached the Final of the 1995 World Youth Cup.

GROUP A

Morocco

ROAD TO FRANCE

Morocco 4 Sierra Leone 0 (9 November 1996)	Sierra Leone 0 Morocco 1 (26 April 1997)
Ghana 2 Morocco 2 (12 January 1997)	Morocco 1 Ghana 0 (7 June 1997)
Gabon 0 Morocco 4 (6 April 1997)	Morocco 2 Gabon 0 (17 August 1997)

WORLD CUP RECORD

First qualified for the finals back in Mexico in 1970, but by the time they had managed a 1-1 draw with Bulgaria they were out – having lost 2-1 to Germany and 3-0 to Peru. It was to be another 16 years before Morocco were back in the finals – and once again it was Mexico. This time they fared much better in their group, drawing 0-0 with Poland, 0-0 with England and then crushing Portugal 3-1. That was good enough to take them through to the last 16 where, after putting up a terrific fight, they were beaten 1-0 by eventual finalists West Germany. There was no such happy outcome from the trip to America in 1994 when they lost all three of their group matches, beaten 1-0 by Belgium, 2-1 by Saudi Arabia and 2-1 by Holland. Regular participants in the African Nations Cup, they have one triumph – in 1976.

KEY PLAYERS

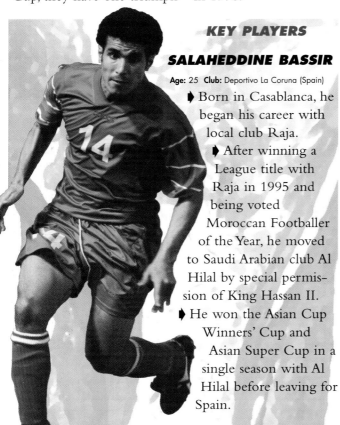

SALAHEDDINE BASSIR

Age: 25 **Club:** Deportivo La Coruna (Spain)

▶ Born in Casablanca, he began his career with local club Raja.

▶ After winning a League title with Raja in 1995 and being voted Moroccan Footballer of the Year, he moved to Saudi Arabian club Al Hilal by special permission of King Hassan II.

▶ He won the Asian Cup Winners' Cup and Asian Super Cup in a single season with Al Hilal before leaving for Spain.

ABDELKRIM HADRIOUI **Age:** 25 **Club:** Benfica (Portugal)

▶ Hadrioui is an attacking left-sided defender.

▶ He provided the cross for the Raghib goal against Ghana which won Morocco's place in France '98.

▶ He made four appearances in the qualifying campaign.

KHALID RAGHIB

Age: 29 **Club:** Settat

▶ He secured Morocco's World Cup place with a goal against Ghana in June 1997.

▶ It was a header in front of 90,000 spectators.

▶ He scored three goals in three qualifying matches.

MANAGER PROFILE

HENRI MICHEL

There will be few coaches in the 1998 World Cup as experienced as Frenchman Henri Michel. Capped 58 times by his country, and a veteran of the 1978 World Cup, he won three French Championships with FC Nantes. In 1982 he switched to coaching and led the French Olympic team to gold in the 1984 Los Angeles Games. He took charge of the French national side and led them to third place in the 1986 World Cup before switching back to club football with Paris St Germain in 1988. A short break followed before working with Cameroon in the 1994 World Cup. A spell in Saudi Arabia came next and then he moved to Morocco. France '98 will be his fourth finals – his third as a coach.

GROUP A

Scotland

ROAD TO FRANCE

Austria 0 Scotland 0 (31 July 1996)	Latvia 0 Scotland 2 (5 October 1996)
Scotland 1 Sweden 0 (10 November 1996)	Estonia 0 Scotland 0 (11 February 1997)
Scotland 2 Estonia 0 (29 March 1997)	Scotland 2 Austria 0 (2 April 1997)
Sweden 2 Scotland 1 (30 April 1997)	Belarus 0 Scotland 1 (6 June 1997)
Scotland 4 Belarus 1 (6 September 1997)	Scotland 2 Latvia 0 (11 October 1997)

WORLD CUP RECORD

In the last 24 years Scotland have outstripped England with their World Cup qualifying successes – appearing in five finals to England's three, and that is reason enough for their fans to cheer. But the time has come for something more. It is a weary old fact – but all the same a fact – that in the seven finals in which they have played a part, Scotland have never been beyond the first round. There have been some good results and some stinkers – their experiences of Argentina in 1978 encapsulating the entire Scottish misfortune. They lost 3-1 to Peru, drew 1-1 with Iran and then beat eventual finalists Holland 3-2. This was the era of great Dutch football played by the likes of Haan, Neeskens, Rensenbrink and Krol and for Scotland the result was almost as good as winning the competition. The feeling persists that if they get past Round One the atmosphere will become heady – and who knows what might happen then?

MANAGER	CRAIG BROWN
PROFILE	Craig Brown has done the easy bit, reaching France, but the hard bit is still to come. Brown, the No. 2 to former coach Andy Roxburgh, took charge in 1993 and his promotion signalled a sensational rise for a man who was once

a schoolteacher and has not played the game at the top level. Brown sends out teams to play in a fast British style and has fashioned a competitive and disciplined side from a base of players who, while proficient, do not boast exotic abilities. Brown has played on typical Scottish strengths, a tough man who evokes unfailing loyalty from his players.

KEY PLAYERS

COLIN HENDRY Age: 32 Club: Blackburn Rovers (England)
- He won a Premiership medal with Blackburn in 1995.
- He cost manager Kenny Dalglish only £700,000 when he moved back to Ewood Park after two years at Manchester City.
- A blond, fearsome defender, Hendry won his first Scottish cap in 1993 against Estonia.

JOHN COLLINS

Age: 29 Club: Monaco (France)
- Collins was the first British footballer to be transferred to the continent under the Bosman ruling, although Celtic valued him at £3 million.
- He is a free-kick specialist.
- He was born in the Borders town of Galashiels, known more as a Rugby Union stronghold.

KEVIN GALLACHER

Age 31. Club: Blackburn Rovers (England)
- Gallacher suffered two broken legs while at Blackburn, the second in his comeback match from the first injury which happened against Arsenal in 1994.
- He wears contact lenses and has played blind, having lost them while on the pitch.
- He was crucial to the qualifying campaign scoring seven goals to take Scotland to France '98.

GROUP A

Norway

ROAD TO FRANCE

Norway 5 Azerbaijan 0 (2 June 1996)	**Norway 3 Hungary 0** (9 October 1996)
Switzerland 0 Norway 1 (10 November 1996)	**Norway 1 Finland 1** (30 April 1997)
Hungary 1 Norway 1 (8 June 1997)	**Finland 0 Norway 4** (20 August 1997)
Azerbaijan 0 Norway 1 (6 September 1997)	**Norway 5 Switzerland 0** (11 October 1997)

WORLD CUP RECORD

The book on Norway's major international footballing exploits is not very thick – they played in the 1938 and 1994 World Cup finals and have never made the European Championship finals. Even so, the 1990s have coincided with a rise in their world status and they are a side expected to cause an upset or two. Back in 1938 in France, the World Cup was played in a straight knockout format and Norway went down 2-1 to Italy, the eventual champions, in the first round. In 1994 they played in a four-team group which finished with all sides boasting a win, a defeat and a draw, but a single goal scored and one goal conceded meant that Norway were eliminated on goal difference. Coach Egil Olsen has tightened up the side and used just 23 players in the eight qualifying matches. A record of six wins and two draws in qualifying marked them out as a team head and shoulders above the rest of their group.

MANAGER	*EGIL OLSEN*
PROFILE	

Egil Olsen is a man who believes in doing his homework – he has a comprehensive database on all his side's matches and directs his team to play in an efficient and effective manner. It has not made him popular, but ever a pragmatist, he realizes all-out attacking football comes at a price. Capped 16 times by Norway, Olsen coached the Norweigan Olympic team from 1979 to 1985, moved to run the Under-21s and then in 1990 was made national coach. Two World Cup finals and a near-miss on qualification for the 1996 Euro Championship have marked him out as a coach who can lead Norway to heights they have never previously reached.

KEY PLAYERS

JAHN IVAR JAKOBSEN Age: 32 Club: Rosenborg

▶ Jakobsen is an all-action player but is relatively small, which has earned him the nickname 'Mini' with his international team-mates.

▶ He has won six Norwegian league titles with Rosenborg as well as three Norwegian Cups, most recently in 1996.

▶ He made his international debut against Bulgaria way back in August 1988 and has since won over 60 caps.

OYVIND LEONHARDSEN

Age: 27 Club: Liverpool (England)

▶ Leonhardsen won three consecutive Norwegian titles between 1992 and 1994 with former club Rosenborg before joining Wimbledon for £600,000.

▶ It was Leonhardsen's goal against Switzerland in Berne that put Norway top of Group Three during their World Cup qualifying campaign.

▶ He joined Liverpool in the summer of 1997 for £4.5 million, a move which saw him link up with England midfielder Paul Ince.

OLE GUNNAR SOLSKJAER

Age: 25 Club: Manchester United (England)

▶ Solskjaer made an immediate impact at Manchester United after signing from Molde FK and finished his first season as the club's leading Premiership scorer.

▶ His youthful appearance and natural goalscoring ability have earned him the nickname of the Baby-Faced Assassin, a title he is known to hate.

▶ He was born in the small fishing port of Kristiansund. His father Oivind is a former professional wrestler.

GROUP B

Italy

ROAD TO FRANCE

Moldova 1 Italy 3 (5 October 1996)	Georgia 0 Italy 0 (10 September 1997)
Italy 1 Georgia 0 (9 October 1996)	Italy 0 England 0 (11 October 1997)
England 0 Italy 1 (12 February 1997)	Italy 3 Moldova 0 (29 March 1997)
Poland 0 Italy 0 (2 April 1997)	Italy 3 Poland 0 (30 April 1997)
PLAY-OFF	
Russia 1 Italy 1 (29 October 1997)	Italy 1 Russia 0 (15 November 1997)

WORLD CUP RECORD

What was different about the 1958 World Cup? The answer: Italy did not play in it. Apart from the 1930 tournament this was the only one they have missed – although reaching France '98 was a close squeeze, Italy making it via a play-off with Russia. Italy are undoubtedly one of the great World Cup countries, with five appearances in the Final and three wins. Their last Final appearance was in America four years ago where they lost on penalties to Brazil.

They first collected the trophy in 1934 when they beat Czechoslovakia 2-1 in Rome thanks to a late equalizer which forced extra-time. Four years later Italy successfully defended their prize with a 4-2 win over Hungary. There was no doubt that with Ferrari and Meazza anchoring the side from midfield, Italy were the side of their era and were only prevented from claiming greater glory by the outbreak of the Second World War. They reached the 1970 Final in Mexico but were overwhelmed 4-1 by Brazil.

It was 12 years before their next Final – in Spain – carried there by stars like Conti, Tardelli, Gentile and Rossi. Three draws in the 1982 qualifying rounds led to an impressive second-round group where Argentina and Brazil were beaten. Poland were beaten 2-0 in the semi-final and then West Germany were crushed in the Final as Italy built up a cosy 3-0 lead. The defence of the trophy in 1986 ended when France won 2-0 in their last-16 clash while 1990 – played again on home soil – ended in a penalty shoot-out semi-final defeat by Argentina. America proved more fruitful as Nigeria, Spain and Bulgaria were beaten to set up a final with arch-rivals Brazil. A dull match ended 0-0 and went to penalties. When Roberto Baggio missed with Italy's fifth penalty, Brazil became the unofficial kings of World Cup football with four wins to Italy's three.

KEY PLAYERS

PAOLO MALDINI Age: 29 Club: AC Milan

- Maldini has played for Milan throughout his whole career, making over 350 appearances.
- His father, Cesare, is coach of the Italian national team and played 14 times for Italy.
- Maldini was voted World Player of the Year in 1994.

DEMETRIO ALBERTINI

Age: 26 Club: AC Milan

- He has won more than 50 Italian caps.
- Albertini played in all of Italy's World Cup final games in USA '94.
- He has won four championship and two European Cup medals.

GIANFRANCO ZOLA

Age: 31 Club: Chelsea (England)

- Zola learned his trade as a free-kick specialist under the tutorship of Maradona at Naples.
- He scored the goal that beat England at Wembley in February, jeopardizing their chances of qualifying.
- He won the 1997 Footballer of the Year award in England after less than one season with Chelsea.

MANAGER *CESARE MALDINI*

PROFILE

As a player, Cesare Maldini collected four championships and a European Cup with AC Milan, but despite this success won just 14 caps. He moved into coaching with Foggia, Terni and then Parma before being drafted in to help with the national side as an assistant to Enzo Bearzot, who masterminded the 1982 World Cup triumph. Maldini coached the Under-21 side to three European titles between 1992 and 1996 before he was asked to take Italy to the France '98 finals in December 1996.

GROUP B

Cameroon

ROAD TO FRANCE

Togo 2 Cameroon 4 (10 November 1996)   Cameroon 0 Angola 0 (12 January 1997)
Cameroon 1 Zimbabwe 0 (6 April 1997)   Cameroon 2 Togo 0 (27 April 1997)
Angola 1 Cameroon 1 (8 June 1997)   Zimbabwe 1 Cameroon 2 (17 August 1997)

WORLD CUP RECORD

The emergence of Africa as a continent with great footballing potential was signalled by the arrival of Cameroon on the world stage back in 1982. Prior to France '98 Cameroon had qualified for the World Cup finals three times and, bar a collapse in 1994, have distinguished themselves. Back in Spain at their debut finals, they drew 0-0 with Peru, 0-0 with Poland and 1-1 with Italy. This was not enough to take them through to the second stage, but by their next appearance, in Italy in 1990, they had come on in leaps and bounds. They stunned world football with a 1-0 win over defending champions Argentina and then saw off Romania 2-1. In the last 16 they beat Colombia 2-1 and were only knocked out in the quarter-finals by England, going down 3-2 in extra-time after conceding two penalties. In America four years ago they started with a 2-2 draw with Sweden, but a 3-0 defeat by Brazil led to a collapse in their spirit and they were hammered 6-1 by Russia in the final group match.

KEY PLAYERS

PATRICK MBOMA Age: 27 Club: Gamba Osaka (Japan)

▶ Mboma's family emigrated from Douala, Cameroon, to France when Mboma was two years old.
▶ He started his career with Chateauroux, later joining Paris St Germain and Metz.
▶ He obtained a French passport, but six goals for Cameroon made him leading scorer in the World Cup qualifying tournament.

SALOMAN OLEMBE Age: 17 Club: Nantes (France)

▶ He became the youngest opponent ever to face England in a senior Wembley international when introduced as substitute during a 2-0 defeat in November, at the age of 16 years 342 days.
▶ Olembe wears size six boots.
▶ When he appeared against England he had played only three first-team matches for Nantes, who were so eager to protect their prodigy they sent a party of escorts to whisk him back to France immediately after the match.

JACQUES SONGO'O

Age: 33 Club: Deportivo La Coruna (Spain)
▶ Songo'o made his Cameroon debut against Angola in the 1983 Olympic qualifier.
▶ His only appearance in two World Cup finals series was a 6-1 defeat by Russia in San Francisco.
▶ He spent five years in France playing for Toulon, Le Mans and Metz.

MANAGER

PROFILE

JEAN MANGA ONGUENE

Jean Manga Onguene was the assistant to Valeri Nepomniachi, who was at the helm for the successful 1990 campaign. Onguene took charge in July 1997 having served a thorough apprenticeship. An international with a career spanning 14 years from 1966–80, he played for Canon Yaounde and, after retiring, earned a coaching badge before joining the national team staff and progressing through the ranks.

GROUP B

Austria

ROAD TO FRANCE

WORLD CUP RECORD

In the beginning Austria were a feared world power in football. One of the 13 nations invited to contest the first competition, they reached the semi-final of the 1934 World Cup where they lost 1-0 to Italy. Then in a play-off for third place they were beaten 3-2 by Germany. By the time Austria next appeared in the finals they had to do it via qualifying. Once in Switzerland in 1954 they did their stuff, coming through the first round at a canter to meet the host nation in what must be one of the most remarkable World Cup matches ever. The score after 90 minutes: Austria 7 Switzerland 5. In the semi-final Austria lost 6-1 to Germany, but picked up third place via the play-off when they defeated Uruguay 3-1. Four years later they were on the plane back home from Sweden after failing to get through the first round.

There followed 20 years in the wilderness before a return to the finals stage in Argentina in 1978, where they reached the second round. Here they were outclassed 5-1 by Holland and lost 1-0 to Italy before saving face with a 3-2 win over rivals West

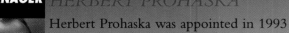

Germany. Spain, in 1982, saw them reach the second stage again, but a 1-0 defeat by France and a 2-2 draw with Northern Ireland ended their interest. Hosts Italy beat them 1-0 in 1990 and the Austrians also lost by the same score to Czechoslovakia. The only consolation was a 2-1 win over the USA.

KEY PLAYERS

TONI POLSTER

Age: 33 **Club:** FC Cologne (Germany)

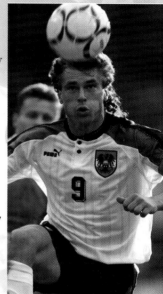

- Depending on the number of friendlies played by Austria before the World Cup finals, Polster is on course to break Gerhard Hanappi's record of 93 appearances during France '98.
- He is the greatest Austrian goalscorer of all time, with 41 goals in 87 appearances.
- He won the European Golden Boot award in 1987, while playing for Austria Vienna.

ANDREAS HERZOG

Age: 29 **Club:** Werder Bremen (Germany)

- Herzog was signed by Werder from Bayern Munich in 1996.
- He had an operation on a recurring toe injury in October 1997.
- He scored the crucial goals in both Austria's 1-0 qualifying victories over Sweden.

MICHAEL KONSEL

Age: 35 **Club:** Roma (Italy)

- Konsel was sent off during a World Cup qualifier v Sweden.
- He spent 12 years with Rapid Vienna, winning consecutive League Championships in 1987 and 1988.
- He has been voted the most consistent keeper in Italy's Serie A.

MANAGER — *HERBERT PROHASKA*

PROFILE

Herbert Prohaska was appointed in 1993 but it was too late to squeeze Austria through to the last World Cup. But he has made it for France and has a talented squad to hand. Prohaska, a player with Inter Milan and AS Roma in the late 1970s, has earned a reputation for producing exciting football teams. He has also coached Austria Vienna.

GROUP B

Chile

ROAD TO FRANCE

Venezuela 1 Chile 1 (2 June 1996)	Chile 4 Ecuador 1 (6 July 1996)
Colombia 4 Chile 1 (1 September 1996)	Paraguay 2 Chile 1 (9 October 1996)
Chile 1 Uruguay 0 (12 November 1996)	Argentina 1 Chile 1 (15 December 1996)
Peru 2 Chile 1 (12 January 1997)	Bolivia 1 Chile 1 (12 February 1997)
Chile 6 Venezuela 0 (29 April 1997)	Ecuador 1 Chile 1 (8 June 1997)
Chile 4 Colombia 1 (5 July 1997)	Chile 2 Paraguay 1 (20 July 1997)
Uruguay 1 Chile 0 (20 August 1997)	Chile 1 Argentia 2 (10 September 1997)
Chile 4 Peru 0 (12 October 1997)	Chile 3 Bolivia 0 (16 November 1997)

WORLD CUP RECORD

Invited to the first party in 1930, it was to be another 20 years and the World Cup of 1950 in Uruguay before Chile reappeared. Their interest did not last that long; they were beaten 2-0 by England and Spain. It was different in 1962 when Chile were hosts. They scored impressive group wins over Switzerland, beaten 3-1, and Italy, defeated 2-0. Then in the quarter-finals the USSR were sent packing 2-1 before Chile faced Brazil. The home team went down 4-2 but regrouped to win the play-off with Yugoslavia for a best-ever finish of third. In England in 1966 they disappeared without a whimper and the same happened in West Germany in 1974. It was to be eight years before their next qualification – this time in Spain where they lost all three of their group matches. France '98 represents Chile's first finals for 16 years.

MANAGER *NELSON ACOSTA*

PROFILE Nelson Acosta was born in Uruguay and featured in local football before taking on a coaching job with Fernandez Vial de Concepcion. He progressed to Chile and Union Espanola and was made Chilean coach at the start of the qualifying campaign for France '98. A man who favours counter-attacking as his chief tactic, he is blessed with two of the best strikers in the world, Marcelo Salas and Ivan Zamorano.

KEY PLAYERS

SEBASTIAN ROZENTAL

Age: 21 **Club:** Glasgow Rangers (Scotland)

▶ Rozental made his debut for Chile aged just 17 and became a regular in the team, until injury prevented him from playing for much of the 1996-97 season.

▶ He signed for Glasgow Rangers in a £4 million deal in January 1997 and impressed everyone with his skill and pace before twisting his knee on his home debut against St Johnstone.

▶ He could prove to be one of the surprises of France '98.

MARCELO SALAS

Age: 22 **Club:** River Plate (Argentina)

▶ Salas scored in the 3-0 victory over Bolivia that secured Chile's place at France '98.

▶ He has already become an automatic choice up front for his country and delighted fans with a first-half hat-trick in the 4-1 victory over Colombia.

▶ He became the target of a number of top European teams, with Lazio winning the race to sign him.

IVAN ZAMORANO **Age:** 30 **Club:** Inter Milan (Italy)

▶ Zamorano has paired up with Salas to form a formidable striking force for the Chilean team.

▶ Not only a provider for Salas, Zamorano is also a lethal finisher in his own right, scoring five in the 6-0 victory over Venezuela.

▶ After winning the Spanish championship with Real Madrid, he moved to Inter Milan in 1996.

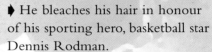

GROUP C

France

WORLD CUP RECORD

The time has come, they feel in France, for the cockerel to strut on the Final stage. Three times France have reached the semi-finals, and three times they have failed to go any further. The first time was back in 1958 when they faced mission impossible – a clash with Brazil. They lost 5-2 but recovered to win the third-place play-off against West Germany 6-3.

There were some barren years, but then in the 1980s, inspired by the remarkable Michel Platini, France became a force. They won the European Championship in 1984, two years after reaching their second World Cup semi-final. The 1982 tournament in Spain saw France recover from a 3-1 group defeat by England to beat Austria and Northern Ireland for a semi-final with West Germany. A cracking match ended 3-3 and went to penalties. Germany, as they have done so many times down the years, won it 5-4 and the crushed French then lost 3-2 in the play-off with Poland.

Mexico in 1986 saw France sail through the group stage for a knockout run that was, on paper, awesome. In the last 16 they faced Italy – and beat them 2-0. Then in the quarter-final Brazil – and beat them 4-3 on penalties after a 1-1 draw. West Germany were next, but France caught a cold and were beaten 2-0. Disappointed and with a squad that was getting old, France went into decline, failing to make Italy and the USA. Aime Jacquet, however, has sorted it out and got France playing again. They went through a 30-match unbeaten run and then reached the semi-finals of Euro '96 in England, where they were beaten by the Czech Republic.

Disappointing though that was, France have restored their confidence and, spurred by national expectation and no little skill, have become leading contenders to win the World Cup in their own backyard – a feat that used to be commonplace but has not happened since Argentina in 1978.

KEY PLAYERS

IBRAHIM BA

Age: 25 **Club:** AC Milan (Italy)

▶ He bleaches his hair in honour of his sporting hero, basketball star Dennis Rodman.

▶ He was handed the awesome responsibility in the 1997–98 season of replacing the legendary Franco Baresi at AC Milan.

▶ He was born in Senegal, where his father was an international player.

DIDIER DESCHAMPS

Age: 29 **Club:** Juventus (Italy)

▶ Eric Cantona called him 'the water carrier' because of his amazing stamina.

▶ He is the midfield anchorman, scoring only 16 goals in 12 seasons with Nantes, Marseille, Bordeaux and Juventus.

▶ He is one of the few players to have won the European Cup with different clubs – Marseille in 1993 and Juventus in 1996.

ZINEDINE ZIDANE

Age: 26 **Club:** Juventus (Italy)

▶ Dennis Bergkamp rates him the best player in Europe.

▶ Zidane was the midfield general behind Juventus reaching the 1996 and 1997 Champions' League Finals.

▶ He was blamed for France's failure in Euro '96 after a series of below-par performances.

MANAGER · AIME JACQUET

PROFILE

As a player Aime Jacquet won just two French caps – hardly a wealth of international experience. But he proved himself at club level with AS Saint-Etienne where, in a 12-year career, the club won five championships and three French Cups. His coaching career started with Olympique Lyonnais, then moved on to Bordeaux, Montpellier and Nancy. He led Bordeaux to three French titles. Appointed to the national coaching squad in the 1992–93 season, 56-year-old Jacquet succeeded Gerard Houllier in December 1993.

GROUP C

Saudi Arabia

ROAD TO FRANCE

Saudi Arabia 2 Kuwait 1 (14 September 1997)   Iran 1 Saudi Arabia 1 (19 September 1997)
China 1 Saudi Arabia 0 (3 October 1997)   Saudia Arabia 1 Qatar 0 (11 October 1997)
Kuwait 2 Saudi Arabia 1 (17 October 1997) Saudi Arabia 1 Iran 0 (24 October 1997)
Saudi Arabia 1 China 1 (6 November 1997)   Qatar 0 Saudi Arabia 1 (12 November 1997)

WORLD CUP RECORD

Saudi Arabia reached their first World Cup finals in the USA in 1994, but they were far from nervous debutants. Drawn in Group F along with Holland, Belguim and Morocco, Saudi proceeded to do well enough to reach the last 16. They were beaten 2-1 in their first finals match – by Holland – but then upset Morocco 2-1 and secured their place in the knockout rounds with an impressive 1-0 victory over Belgium. The next match was against Sweden and they were comprehensively beaten 3-1 by a side destined to reach the semi-finals and then win the 3rd-place Final. Football was not played in Saudi Arabia until the late 1950s, when it was imported by European immigrants moving there to work in the booming oil industry. Developed with the help of Brazilian coaches, the country did not entertain World Cup hopes until 1978. Their performance in the USA was very much against the odds.

KEY PLAYERS

KHALIL AL MUWALID

Age: 26 **Club:** Al Ahli

▶ He has 86 caps.
▶ He scored the crucial penalty in the 1996 Asian Cup Final against United Arab Emirates.
▶ He has a reputation for being a midfield dynamo.

HUSSAIN SULIMANI

Age: 20 **Club:** Al Ahli

▶ He was sent off for handball in the 86th minute of the 1996 Asian Cup Final.
▶ Sulimani already has 35 caps under his belt.
▶ He is the youngest player in the squad and is reputedly his manager's favourite.

MANAGER

ALBERTO PARREIRA

PROFILE

Alberto Parreira is a winner. He was in charge of Brazil when they won in the USA four years ago. This time he goes to the World Cup determined to enjoy the experience and with reaching the second round his main aim. Qualification was won by Otto Pfister, a German who has been in Africa for the majority of his coaching life, working his way up to bigger and better things. Pfister coached Rwanda, Burkina-Faso, Senegal, the Ivory Coast, Zaire and Ghana. He took Ghana to the final of the 1992 African Nations Cup, and was only appointed by Saudi in 1997.

MOHOMMED AL-DAEYEA

Age: 25 **Club:** Al Tae

▶ He has 89 caps.
▶ He kept Saudia Arabia in the Asian Cup Final with some brilliant saves.
▶ He was beaten three times in a friendly with Germany in February '97.

GROUP C

Denmark

ROAD TO FRANCE

Slovenia 0 Denmark 2 (1 September 1996)	Denmark 2 Greece 1 (9 October 1996)
Croatia 1 Denmark 1 (29 March 1997)	Denmark 4 Slovenia 0 (30 April 1997)
Denmark 2 Bosnia 0 (8 June 1997)	Bosnia 3 Denmark 0 (20 August 1997)
Denmark 3 Croatia 1 (10 September 1997)	Greece 0 Denmark 0 (11 October 1997)

WORLD CUP RECORD

It is strange, given the international reputation of some of their players – the likes of the Laudrup brothers, Brian and Michael, and goalkeeper Peter Schmeichel – that Denmark have only once reached the finals of the World Cup, back in 1986. They started off in Mexico that year like a team possessed, romping through their group matches with a 1-0 win over Scotland, 6-1 over Uruguay and 2-0 over eventual finalists Germany. It then went wrong in the last 16 as Spain demolished them 5-1. Since then Denmark have been in the wilderness of world football, with one exception. Invited to join the 1992 European Championship at late notice, they then went on to win the competition. With a growing belief in their abilities and with players making waves in European football, Denmark have the potential to make a serious challenge and will be a side watched warily by all others.

MANAGER	BO JOHANSSON

The groundwork was done by Sepp Piontek in the 1986 World Cup finals, but Bo Johansson has taken Denmark forward, to build on the 1992 European Championship. He is obviously not afraid of learning from anyone – in 1996 Johansson brought his entire backroom staff over to England to watch Wimbledon in action. His challenge in France will start at the back with the commanding presence of Peter Schmeichel in goal, and that should give the defence plenty of confidence. From there his side have plenty of skill with the Laudrup brothers, particularly Michael who, although fast heading towards his mid-thirties, is still performing.

PROFILE

KEY PLAYERS

BRIAN LAUDRUP

Age: 29 Club: Chelsea (England)

▶ Laudrup has played top-flight club football in four European countries so far– Denmark, Germany, Italy and Scotland.

▶ He proved an instant hit at Rangers following his move from AC Milan in the summer of 1994. In his first season in Scotland he was voted Footballer of the Year as Rangers lifted the championship.

▶ He ended his self-imposed exile from the national team in time to be a part of the Denmark side which won the 1992 European Championship in Sweden.

MICHAEL LAUDRUP

Age: 33 Club: Ajax (Holland)

▶ Like father Finn and younger brother Brian, Michael is a Denmark international and the country's Footballer of the Year.

▶ He is the one surviving member of Denmark's only previous trip to the World Cup finals. Back in 1986, he scored one of the tournament's most memorable goals in the 6-1 drubbing of Uruguay.

▶ A dispute with then Denmark coach Richard Moller Nielsen led to him missing 29 internationals, including the 1992 European Championship.

PETER SCHMEICHEL Age: 34 Club: Manchester United (England)

▶ Schmeichel has won English championships and FA Cups since moving to Manchester United from Brondby in the summer of 1991.

▶ He played a key role in Denmark's greatest moment, their 2-0 European Championship final success over Germany in Sweden in 1992.

▶ He won his 97th cap for Denmark in the vital 0-0 draw in Greece, which ensured qualification for France '98.

GROUP C

South Africa

ROAD TO FRANCE

Malawi 0 South Africa 1 (1 June 1996)	**South Africa 3 Malawi 0** (15 June 1996)
South Africa 1 Zaire 0 (9 November 1996)	**Zambia 0 South Africa 0** (12 January 1997)
Congo 2 South Africa 0 (6 April 1997)	**Zaire 1 South Africa 2** (27 April 1997)
South Africa 3 Zambia 0 (8 June 1997)	**South Africa 1 Congo 0** (17 August 1997)

WORLD CUP RECORDS

This is South Africa's first appearance in the World Cup finals, but it comes as no surprise given the surge of African football in the last 12 years. Along with Cameroon and Nigeria, South Africa breathe fresh life into the tournament and will play with an innocence that could catch some of the established powers off guard. There is no telling what they will achieve, although given the successes of other African nations, there will be a sense of trepidation from their rivals. The best yardstick for measuring their advance is the fact that on their first entry into the African Nations Cup, they won the competition, beating Tunisia 2-0 in Johannesburg back in 1996. They were far from disgraced when they lost 2-1 against England at Old Trafford in 1997.

MANAGER	*PHILIPPE TROUSSIER*
PROFILE	Troussier was unable to start his job until the March before the '98 finals, but believed he could bring fresh blood to South Africa. He has managed Ivory Coast, Nigeria, Burkina Faso and was in charge of the South African club side Kaizer Chiefs for nine months in 1994. French born, he saw out his contract with Burkina before moving on to his World Cup duties.

KEY PLAYERS

MARK FISH

Age: 24 **Club:** Bolton (England)

▶ Fish became Bolton's joint record signing when he joined the Wanderers for £2.5 million from Lazio in August 1996.

▶ He was South Africa's youngest cap when he played against Mexico in October 1993, at the age of only 19.

▶ His hero is Marcel Desailly, whom he played alongside when he was chosen to appear in a FIFA World XI team against Brazil two years ago.

PHILOMEN MASINGA **Age:** 28 **Club:** Bari (Italy)

▶ Masinga spent two years with Leeds United, scoring ten goals and earning the nickname of 'Waltzing Masinga'.

▶ He had a brief 'retirement' from international football, upset that he had been abused by home fans.

▶ He scored four goals in South Africa's World Cup qualifying campaign, including the goal against Congo which booked their passage to France.

JOHN MOSHOEU

Age: 32 **Club:** Kocaelispor (Turkey)

▶ Moshoeu's bicycle kick set up Masinga's goal when the South Africans played England at Old Trafford. Such tricks have brought him the nickname of 'Shoes'.

▶ He helped his club to a shock victory in the 1997 Turkish Cup, earning them a place in Europe.

▶ Moshoeu started his career at Blackpool; not the English Second Division club but his local team in Dobsonville, Johannesburg.

GROUP D

Nigeria

ROAD TO FRANCE

Nigeria 2 Burkina Faso 0 (9 November 1996) | Kenya 1 Nigeria 1 (12 January 1997)
Nigeria 2 Guinea 1 (5 April 1997) | Burkina Faso 1 Nigeria 2 (27 April 1997)
Nigeria 3 Kenya 0 (7 June 1997) | Guinea 1 Nigeria 0 (17 August 1997)

WORLD CUP RECORD

The coming face of soccer, Nigeria have only once reached the finals – in 1994 – where they made the last 16 before losing 2-1 to Italy in extra-time. They reached that stage after beating Greece 2-0 and eventual semi-finalists Bulgaria 3-0 in the group rounds in America. That is not a bad record, and a further reason for expecting great things of Nigeria is the fact that they are the current Olympic champions, beating Argentina in the 1996 Final. That tournament was geared towards young players and it suggests that there is a con-siderable amount of emerging talent in the country. There have been triumphs on their own continent with two wins in the African Nations Cup: Nigeria beat Algeria in 1980 and Zambia in 1994.

MANAGER **PROFILE** *BORA MILUTINOVIC*

After much speculation and with Terry Venables' name in the frame, Nigeria even-tually plumped for sacked Mexico coach Bora Milutinovic. He has done wonders with countries ranked as outsiders. As a player, Serbian-born Bora played for Partizan Belgrade before continuing his career in Switzerland, France and then Mexico, where he moved into coaching after his playing days ended. He was in charge of Mexico in 1986 when they reached the quarter-finals and he was at the helm of the USA side which surprised everyone by making the last 16 in 1994. Milutinovic replaces Amadu Shuaibu who was the surprise choice to succeed the Dutchman Clemens Westerhof in late 1994.

KEY PLAYERS

DANIEL AMOKACHI Age: 25 Club: Besiktas (Turkey)

◆ When Everton beat Manchester United in the 1995 FA Cup Final, the game was broadcast live in Nigeria for the first time because Amokachi came on as a sub.
◆ His big break came when he went on a tour to Holland with Nigeria when he was just 17. Bruges spotted him and signed him from his hometown club Ranchers Bees.
◆ He was close to signing for Juventus in 1994, but the deal fell through and he had to join Everton, who gave him a three-year deal worth £2 million.

SUNDAY OLISEH

Age: 23 Club: Ajax (Holland)

◆ Oliseh left home at the age of 16 to join Belgian club FC Liege, where he was first noticed by Nigeria's coach Clemens Westerhof.
◆ In the 1994 World Cup, it was Oliseh's sloppy throw-in that allowed Italy to score the equalizer and prevent one of the tournament's biggest shocks.

◆ In the 1996–97 season, while playing with FC Cologne, he was named as the best defensive midfield-er in the Bundesliga.

FINIDI GEORGE

Age: 27 Club: Real Betis (Spain)

◆ George was voted best player in Holland during his spell with Ajax, where he won three Champion-ships and a Champions' League title.
◆ He left Ajax for Spanish side Real Betis because he found his club-mates at the Dutch club cold and aloof.
◆ George played in all Nigeria's matches in USA '94, scoring against Greece.

GROUP D

Bulgaria

ROAD TO FRANCE

Israel 1 Bulgaria 2 (1 September 1996)	Luxembourg 1 Bulgaria 2 (8 October 1996)
Cyprus 1 Bulgaria 3 (14 December 1996)	Bulgaria 4 Cyprus 1 (2 April 1997)
Bulgaria 4 Luxembourg 0 (8 June 1997)	Bulgaria 1 Israel 0 (20 August 1997)
Bulgaria 1 Russia 0 (10 September 1997)	Russia 4 Bulgaria 2 (11 October 1997)

WORLD CUP RECORD

Bulgaria have appeared in six World Cup finals, the first in 1962, but it wasn't until the finals in the USA in 1994 that they finally managed to win a game. Having done so, however, they forged through to the semi-finals, eventually losing the third-place Final. The East Europeans have certainly made something of an impact in recent years, and with the likes of Letchkov and Stoitchkov in their ranks have one of the most potent attacking midfield pairings in world football. Back in 1986 they drew 1-1 with defending World Champions Italy in their first match and had another 1-1 draw in the next game against South Korea. A 2-0 defeat by eventual champions Argentina could not stop Bulgaria reaching the last 16 where they were beaten 2-0 by Mexico.

In America four years ago, Bulgaria were the tournament's shock side. Hammered 3-0 in their opening group match against Nigeria, they then beat Greece 4-0 and Argentina 2-0. They reached the quarter-finals after a 1-1 draw with Mexico was settled on penalties. Then they faced Germany and produced one of the shocks of the competition, beating the World Champions 2-1. Italy proved too strong in the semi-final, triumphing 2-1 – and in the 3rd-place Final, a disheartened Bulgarian side were hammered 4-0 by Sweden.

MANAGER

PROFILE

HRISTO BONEV

Success has come thanks to a few truly world-class stars finding themselves playing in the same generation. That, however, will soon be a thing of the past if Hristo Bonev has his way. The former Bulgarian striker, with an impressive international record of 47 goals in 96 games, was put in sole charge after Euro '96 and has worked hard to instal a team-ethic in his charges. Demanding fitness levels have been set while players have been carefully coached into a system that is functional rather than immediately dynamic.

KEY PLAYERS

TRIFON IVANOV Age: 32
Club: Rapid Vienna (Austria)

▶ Ivanov is a rugged and aggressive player and fully lives up to his nickname of 'Wolfman'.

▶ He succeeded Hristo Stoitchkov as the national captain after Euro '96.

▶ Ivanov has been a full international for a decade, making his debut against East Germany in 1988.

HRISTO STOITCHKOV Age: 32
Club: Barcelona (Spain)

▶ Stoitchkov refused to play for his country for over a year in protest at the sacking of national coaches Dimitar Penev and Hristo Bonev after a disappointing Euro '96 campaign.

▶ He began his second spell with Barcelona when he signed from Parma in 1996.

▶ He finished the 1994 World Cup finals with six goals, to win the Golden Boot award for the tournament's top scorer and was instrumental in Bulgaria's march to the semi-finals.

YORDAN LETCHKOV Age: 30
Club: Besiktas (Turkey)

▶ Letchkov was another of the senior Bulgarian players who had a year's self-imposed exile from international football in protest at the sacking of Penev and then Bonev.

▶ Like many of his international team-mates he plays outside Bulgaria and transferred from Marseille to Besiktas in July 1997.

▶ He became famous for his diving header in the quarter-finals of the 1994 World Cup in America, which helped knock Germany out of the competition.

GROUP D

Spain

ROAD TO FRANCE

Faroe Islands 2 Spain 6 (4 September 1996)	Spain 4 Malta 0 (12 February 1997)
Czech Republic 0 Spain 0 (9 October 1996)	Yugoslavia 1 Spain 1 (30 April 1997)
Spain 4 Slovakia 1 (13 November 1996)	Spain 1 Czech Republic 0 (8 June 1997)
Spain 2 Yugoslavia 0 (14 December 1996)	Slovakia 1 Spain 2 (24 September 1997)
Malta 0 Spain 3 (18 December 1996)	Spain 3 Faroe Islands 1 (11 October 1997)

WORLD CUP RECORD

They boast one of the most glamorous leagues in the world, yet at international level Spain have not really delivered. By and large Spain have disappointed in the finals, although they had good competitions in 1986 and 1994. A fourth place in 1950 was achieved in a four-group second stage, with the top two teams then contesting the Final. Spain lost 6-1 to Brazil, 3-1 to Sweden and drew 2-2 with Uruguay. Hosts in 1982, they struggled through to the second round-robin stage where they had to play West Germany and England. They lost 2-1 to Germany, the eventual finalists, and drew 0-0 with England. Mexico in 1986 was a great improvement. After an opening match 1-0 defeat by Brazil, Spain picked up the pace, thrashed Denmark 5-1 in the last 16 and were denied a semi-final spot when Belgium beat them on penalties after a 1-1 draw. In America four years ago a 2-2 draw with South Korea did not augur well, but was followed by a 1-1 draw with Germany and a 3-1 defeat of Bolivia. In the last 16 Switzerland were crushed 3-0, but Spain were knocked out 2-1 by Italy, quarter-final winners and eventual finalists.

MANAGER *JAVIER CLEMENTE*

PROFILE

Spain are taking their World Cup very seriously, with coach Javier Clemente able to keep tabs on all his squad because they are involved exclusively in Spanish club football. Javier, a Basque who played for Athletic Bilbao, took up the national coaching job in 1992 after helping Spain to an Olympic gold football medal. Willing to call on young players, Javier – now in his mid-forties – has given the side hope and in return the team embarked on a long unbeaten run following the 1994 World Cup – so impressive that it lifted Spain to second place in the world rankings.

KEY PLAYERS

FERNANDO HIERRO

Age: 30 **Club:** Real Madrid

▶ In Spanish 'Hierro' means 'iron', which is fitting considering the Real Madrid defender is Spain's most notorious hardman.

▶ He was selected for the Spanish squad for the 1990 World Cup finals in Italy but he did not make a single appearance during the tournament.

▶ Hierro has a £21 million contract with Real Madrid which will keep him at the Bernabeu until 2003 and is worth a healthy £1.5 million per year.

LUIS ENRIQUE **Age:** 28 **Club:** Barcelona

▶ Luis Enrique is a genuinely versatile player and can operate in the back four or as an attacking midfielder.

▶ He has a 1993 Spanish Cup and a 1995 Spanish League winner's medal, which he won with his former club Real Madrid, where he spent five seasons.

▶ In a 1997 poll of Barcelona fans, over 70 per cent voted Luis Enrique as the club's 'most valuable player'.

RAUL GONZALEZ **Age:** 21 **Club:** Real Madrid

▶ Raul made his Real Madrid debut in a 5-0 victory over Barcelona and scored his first senior goal for the club against arch-rivals Atletico Madrid – the club he played for as a child.

▶ His greatest ambition outside football is to meet the King of Spain.

▶ He missed out on Euro '96 because, aged 19, he was considered too young. He went to Atlanta instead to help defend Spain's Olympic football title.

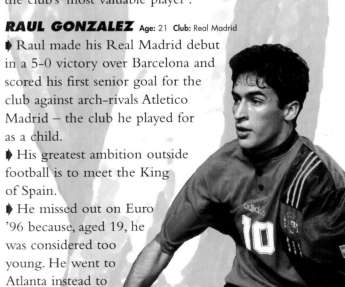

GROUP D

Paraguay

WORLD CUP RECORD

Peru 1 Paraguay 0 (16 March 1997)	Colombia 1 Paraguay 0 (24 April 1996)
Uruguay 0 Paraguay 2 (2 June 1996)	Argentina 1 Paraguay 1 (1 September 1996)
Paraguay 2 Chile 1 (9 October 1996)	Paraguay 1 Venzuela 0 (12 October 1997)
Paraguay 1 Ecuador 0 (10 November 1996)	Bolivia 0 Paraguay 0 (15 December 1996)
Venezuela 0 Paraguay 2 (12 January 1997)	Paraguay 2 Peru 1 (12 February 1997)
Paraguay 2 Colombia 1 (2 April 1997)	Paraguay 2 Uruguay 1 (30 April 1997)
Paraguay 1 Argentina 2 (6 July 1997)	Chile 2 Paraguay 1 (20 July 1997)
Ecuador 2 Paraguay 1 (20 August 1997)	Paraguay 2 Bolivia 1 (10 September 1997)

WORLD CUP RECORD

Four times Paraguay have been in the finals of the World Cup, but they are still waiting to make a significant impact on the tournament. They were invited to the first competition back in 1930, but a 3-0 defeat at the hands of the USA ended their interest. In Brazil 20 years on, they were eliminated after the first round following a 2-2 draw with Sweden and then a 2-0 defeat by Italy. A trip to Sweden in 1958 has been Paraguay's only previous World Cup in Europe. They managed a 1-1 draw with Scotland and a 3-3 draw with Yugoslavia but were hammered 7-3 by France. Paraguay's best moment came in 1986 when a 1-1 draw with host nation Mexico, a 1-0 win over Iraq and a 2-2 draw with Belgium took them through to the knock-out stages for the first time. There they met England and were comprehensively beaten 3-0.

MANAGER PROFILE

PAULO CESAR CARPEGIANI

A firm believer that attack is the best form of defence, Paulo Cesar Carpegiani is a Brazilian who played for Porto Alegre and then Flamengo. He was a member of the Brazilian squad that went to West Germany for the 1974 World Cup. Now in his late forties, he started his coaching career with Flamengo – winners of the 1981 World Club Championship when they beat Liverpool 3-0. He also won a Brazilian League title with the club.

FRANCISCO ARCE

Age: 26 **Club:** Gremio (Brazil)

▶ Arce started his football career as a promising midfielder, but is now one of the best right-backs in South America.
▶ He played at the 1992 Olympics in Barcelona.
▶ Only a penalty shoot-out defeat by Ajax in the World Club Championship has prevented him from a clean sweep of club honours at Gremio.

CARLOS GAMARRA
Age: 26 **Club:** Benfica (Portugal)

▶ He is the star man in the team's defensive back three.
▶ He was joint top-scorer with three goals in the World Cup qualification.
▶ He played for two years with Internacional in Brazil.

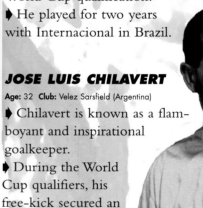

JOSE LUIS CHILAVERT
Age: 32 **Club:** Velez Sarsfield (Argentina)

▶ Chilavert is known as a flamboyant and inspirational goalkeeper.
▶ During the World Cup qualifiers, his free-kick secured an important draw against Argentina in Buenos Aires.
▶ He received a four-match ban for fighting with Tino Asprilla in the match against Colombia in April 1996.

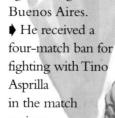

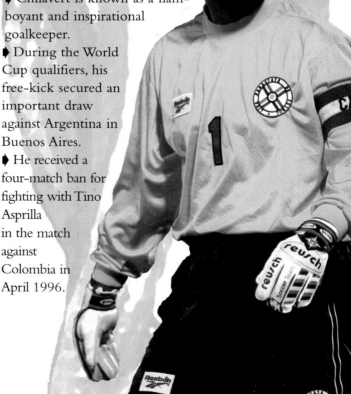

GROUP E

Mexico

ROAD TO FRANCE

Mexico 4 Canada 0 (2 March 1997)
Costa Rica 0 Mexico 0 (16 March 1997)
Mexico 6 Jamaica 0 (13 April 1997)
USA 2 Mexico 2 (20 April 1997)
Jamaica 0 Mexico 0 (16 November 1997)

Mexico 5 El Salvador 0 (5 October 1997)
Canada 2 Mexico 2 (12 October 1997)
Mexico 0 USA 0 (2 November 1997)
Mexico 3 Costa Rica 3 (9 November 1997)

WORLD CUP RECORD

Mexico have a long association with the tournament, dating back to the beginning in 1930, and have twice been quarter-finalists – both times when they have hosted the World Cup. They failed to qualify in 1934, 1974 and 1982, did not enter in 1938 and were banned in 1990, having played over-age players in an international youth tournament. Amazingly, it was not until the 1962 competition that they won a match in the finals stages, when they beat Czechoslovakia 3-1 in Chile. By that stage they had already lost to Brazil and Spain.

Mexico have a reputation for being an up-and-down side, brilliant against some of the best teams in the world and then dismal against outsiders – as in 1978 when they lost 3-1 to 1000-1 Tunisia. In 1970 they reached the last eight where Italy, the eventual finalists, needed extra-time to win 4-1. In 1986 it was West Germany, another country to progress past Mexico only to become beaten finalists, who triumphed – but only after penalties following a 0-0 draw. In the USA in 1994 Mexico reached the last 16 where they played Bulgaria. The match ended 1-1 but was decided in the Bulgarians' favour following a penalty shoot-out.

MANAGER MANUEL LAPUENTE

PROFILE The hard work was done by Bora Milutinovic – a miracle worker who has done wonders with rank outsiders. He was in charge of Mexico in 1986 when they reached the quarter-finals and then the USA, where he took them to the last 16 in 1994. Back with Mexico, he helped them qualify for France – and was then fired after three poor results. Manuel Lapuente, coach of the Mexico City club Necaxa, is now in charge for the second time, having previously been fired in 1992.

KEY PLAYERS

JORGE CAMPOS

Age: 30 **Club:** Los Angeles Galaxy (USA)

▶ Campos helped Mexico win back-to-back CONCACAF Gold Cups in 1993 and 1995, finish runners-up in the 1993 Copa América and reach the last 16 of the 1994 World Cup.
▶ He is known as an 'overlapping goalkeeper' for his regular excursions upfield.
▶ He played most of the 1989 Mexican season as a striker because he could not dislodge the established goalkeeper at UNAM – and finished top scorer for the club with 14 goals.

RAMON RAMIREZ

Age: 27 **Club:** Guadalajara

▶ Without a doubt, Ramirez is the ball-winning fulcrum of the Mexican midfield.
▶ He made 14 qualifying appearances.
▶ He scored against Honduras and Canada as Mexico qualified

CARLOS HERMOSILLO

Age: 33 **Club:** Cruz Azul

▶ He made 14 appearances in Mexico's qualifying campaign.
▶ He scored 10 goals throughout the qualifying tournament.
▶ He ended this campaign two caps short of a century.

GROUP E

South Korea

ROAD TO FRANCE

South Korea 3 Kazakhstan 0 (6 September 1997)	**South Korea 2 Uzbekistan 1** (12 September 1997)
Japan 1 South Korea 2 (28 September 1997)	**South Korea 3 UAE 0** (4 October 1997)
Kazakhstan 1 South Korea 1 (11 October 1997)	**Uzbekistan 1 South Korea 5** (18 October 1997)
South Korea 0 Japan 2 (1 November 1997)	**UAE 1 South Korea 3** (9 November 1997)

WORLD CUP RECORD

In the last 12 years there has been something of a footballing renaissance in South Korea, who are making their fourth successive appearance in the World Cup finals. Until 1986 they had only reached the final stages once before – back in Switzerland in 1954. The Koreans will feel happy that time has made that memory fade, because they lost 9-0 to Hungary and then 7-0 to Turkey. The Hungary defeat was forgivable as it was against the Mighty Magyars; the Hungary of Puskás, Boszik and Kocsis.

By 1986 and the Mexico finals, South Korea had come on in leaps and bounds and they covered themselves with glory, if not winning results. They lost their first match 3-1 to Argentina, the eventual world champions, and drew 1-1 with Bulgaria before losing 3-2 to Italy. The results were not quite so good in Italy for the 1990 World Cup, where they lost all three of their group matches; beaten 2-0 by Belgium, 3-1 by Spain and 1-0 by Uruguay. The trip to the USA for 1994 was much better – there was a 2-2 draw with Spain, a 0-0 draw with Bolivia and a 3-2 defeat by Germany. They are still awaiting their first finals win, but given that they have run the footballing powers of Argentina, Germany and Italy close, the day must surely be close at hand.

MANAGER *CHA BUM-KUN*

PROFILE

Appointed in January 1997 after ten seasons spent working in the German Bundesliga with Bayer Leverkusen and Eintracht Frankfurt, Cha Bum-kun has instilled German standards of efficiency, discipline, fitness and mental strength in his squad. Unbeaten in qualifying, a finals win would be a good enough starting point, but Bum-kun is more ambitious than that.

KEY PLAYERS

CHOI YOUNG-SU

Age: 24 **Club:** Sangmoo

- He was South Korea's leading scorer in World Cup qualification, netting eight goals.
- When South Korea played Japan in November, they lost after Young-su left the field with a nose injury.
- He featured in his country's Olympic team while playing with Lucky Goldstar Cheetahs.

PARK KUN-HA

Age: 26 **Club:** Suwon Bluewings

- He read a declaration of the Bluewings' intentions when they were formed and joined the Korean League in 1995.
- Kun-ha lists listening to music as his favourite hobby.
- His only goals of the World Cup qualifying campaign came in their 4-0 win over Hong Kong.

CHOI YOUNG-IL

Age: 31 **Club:** Pusan Daewoo

- He is one of South Korea's more experienced players, having played over 40 games for his country.
- He helped his club to a shock victory in the Adidas Cup.
- He enjoys watching all kinds of sport, especially NBA basketball.

GROUP E

Belgium

ROAD TO FRANCE

Belgium 2 Turkey 1 (31 August 1996)	**San Marino 0 Belgium 3** (9 October 1996)
Belgium 0 Holland 3 (14 December 1996)	**Wales 1 Belgium 2** (29 March 1997)
Turkey 1 Belgium 3 (30 April 1997)	**Belgium 6 San Marino 0** (7 June 1997)
Holland 3 Belgium 1 (6 September 1997)	**Belgium 3 Wales 2** (11 October 1997)
PLAY-OFF	
Republic of Ireland 1 Belgium 1 (29 October 1997)	**Belgium 2 Republic of Ireland 1** (15 November 1997)

WORLD CUP RECORD

Belgium have been to the World Cup finals party nine times, yet boast a lowly FIFA world ranking of No. 48. They are always tough opponents, but it was not until the Spain World Cup of 1982 that they finally got beyond the opening round – where in a round-robin tournament they lost 3-0 to Poland and 1-0 to the USSR. Revenge was sweet in 1986, however, when they scored a thrilling 4-3 extra-time win over the USSR in Mexico.

In the quarter-final they were up against Spain, drew 1-1 and then triumphed 5-4 in the penalty shoot-out to win a semi-final place against the eventual winners Argentina. They lost the match 2-0.

Four years later they were in the last 16 again, having the better of the match against England. Extra-time was almost over when David Platt's spectacular volleyed winner ended Belgium's tournament in Italy.

In the USA four years ago, Belgium scored a superb group win over Holland, but then lost to Saudi Arabia. They qualified for the last 16 but faced Germany. Despite a good fight they were knocked out 3-2.

KEY PLAYERS

GILLES DE BILDE

Age: 26 **Club:** PSV Eindhoven (Holland)

▶ De Bilde was voted Belgian Footballer of the Year in 1994.

▶ He was banned for three months by the Belgian Football Federation after punching an opponent in December 1996.

▶ In just three months he was instrumental in PSV clinching the Dutch league title with a contribution of seven goals.

ENZO SCIFO

Age: 31 **Club:** Anderlecht

▶ Scifo has played for top European clubs including Anderlecht, Inter, Torino, Bordeaux, Auxerre and Monaco.

▶ He has Italian ancestry.

▶ In the mid-1980s he was Anderlecht's boy wonder.

MARC WILMOTS

Age: 28 **Club:** Schalke (Germany)

▶ Wilmots scored in the semi-final and final of Schalke's surprise UEFA Cup victory in 1997.

▶ He spent a lot of his boyhood helping his father farm the land north of Brussels.

▶ Before moving to the Bundesliga in 1996, Wilmots played for ten years in the Belgian league.

MANAGER	*GEORGE LEEKENS*
PROFILE	A former Bruges defender, George Leekens learned his trade in Belgium, coaching at seven clubs – among them Anderlecht and Bruges. Now in his mid-forties, Leekens was put in charge of the national side early last year and guided

them through to France '98 via a tough group and two tense play-off matches with the Republic of Ireland.

GROUP E

Holland

ROAD TO FRANCE

Wales 1 Holland 3 (5 October 1996)	**Turkey 1 Holland 0** (2 April 1997)
Holland 7 Wales 1 (9 November 1996)	**San Marino 0 Holland 6** (30 April 1997)
Belgium 0 Holland 3 (14 December 1996)	**Holland 3 Belgium 0** (6 September 1997)
Holland 4 San Marino 0 (29 March 1997)	**Holland 0 Turkey 0** (11 October 1997)

WORLD CUP RECORD

Until the 1970s Holland were one of the World Cup also-rans with just one appearance – in 1934. When they re-emerged in the 1974 World Cup in West Germany, they were to take football by the scruff of the neck and transform it into a pure game. Total Football was the Dutch way and with the likes of Haan, Krol, Neeskens, Rep, Cruyff, Rensenbrink and Van de Kerkhof, they had the players to make it happen. They strolled through the first group stages and played even better in the next super group round, beating Argentina 4-0, East Germany 2-0 and Brazil 2-0. That earned them a Final against the host nation, West Germany. Within a minute Holland led and they were clearly the better side. But dogged persistence brought Germany into the game and they lifted the trophy with a 2-1 win.

Four years later Holland still had too much for most opponents, and found themselves in a second group stage. A 5-1 win over Austria, a 2-2 draw with West Germany and a 2-1 win against Italy earned them a second successive Final – again facing the host nation, where they lost 3-1 in extra-time.

In 1990 they never really got going, but America proved a happier experience four years ago, until they went down 3-2 to Brazil, the eventual champions, in a pulsating quarter-final.

MANAGER | **GUUS HIDDINK**

PROFILE

Guus Hiddink is true to the Dutch footballing philosophy of playing attractive football. Left with a difficult task of balancing players who are spread all around the globe, Hiddink has had to speak his mind to a group of them. Hiddink spent three seasons coaching Spanish league side Valencia and then had a spell at Fenerbahce. A close friend of Johan Cruyff, the former PSV Eindhoven player coached the Dutch club to the 1988 European Cup.

KEY PLAYERS

CLARENCE SEEDORF

Age: 22 **Club:** Real Madrid (Spain)

▶ A product of the successful Ajax youth policy, Seedorf made his international debut at the age of 18, against Luxembourg in 1994.

▶ He picked up a Champions' League winner's medal in 1995 with Ajax.

▶ He has already been the subject of two £3 million moves, firstly from Ajax to Sampdoria in Italy, and from there on to Real Madrid.

PATRICK KLUIVERT

Age: 21 **Club:** AC Milan (Italy)

▶ Kluivert became an instant sensation as a teenage striker for both Ajax and Holland. He scored the winning goal in the 1995 Champions' League Final.

▶ His double strike in the play-off qualification match against the Republic of Ireland sent Holland to the 1994 World Cup finals in the United States.

▶ He overcame personal problems and the pressures of a high-profile move to AC Milan to help his country again into the World Cup finals with two goals in the key qualifier against Belgium.

DENNIS BERGKAMP

Age: 29 **Club:** Arsenal (England)

▶ Bergkamp has won three European club medals in his career – two UEFA Cups (with Ajax and Inter Milan) and the Cup Winners' Cup with Ajax.

▶ He has a chronic fear of flying and vowed after the 1994 World Cup in the United States never to take to the air again.

▶ He joined Arsenal in July 1995 for £7.5 million and is the first player ever to win successive FA Carling Premiership Player of the Month awards.

GROUP F

Iran

ROAD TO FRANCE

ROUND ONE

Maldives 0 Iran 17 (2 June 1997)
Kyrgyzstan 0 Iran 7 (4 June 1997)
Syria 0 Iran 0 (6 June 1997)
Iran 3 Kyrgyzstan 1 (9 June 1997)
Iran 9 Maldives 0 (11 June 1997)
Iran 2 Syria 2 (13 June 1997)
Iran 0 Kuwait 0 (31 October 1997)

THIRD PLACE

Iran 2 Japan 3 (16 November 1997)

PLAY-OFF

Iran 1 Australia 1 (22 November 1997)

ROUND TWO

China 2 Iran 4 (13 September 1997)
Iran 1 Saudi Arabia 1 (19 September 1997)
Kuwait 1 Iran 1 (26 Sptember 1997)
Iran 3 Qatar 0 (3 October 1997)
Iran 4 China 1 (17 October 1997)
Saudia Arabia 1 Iran 0 (24 October 1997)
Qatar 2 Iran 0 (7 November 1997)

Australia 2 Iran 2 (29 November 1997)

WORLD CUP RECORD

Their one finals appearance before France '98 came in 1978, when Iranian football was at its strongest. They had just won their third Asian Championship in 1976, having held the title twice before, in 1972 and 1968. They went to Argentina and were in a tough group facing Holland, the eventual finalists, Peru and Scotland. They lost 3-0 to Holland and 4-1 to Peru but in between had their moment of glory, a 1-1 draw with Scotland. Encouraged, the next World Cup in Spain in 1982 became a real target, but revolution and war with Iraq pushed football out of the way. When they returned to the Asian Championship in 1988 they came third, a position not bettered – although their sensational play-off qualifying win over Australia, when they came back from 2-0 down in the last 20 minutes in Melbourne to make it 2-2 and qualify on away goals, marks a significant upturn in the fortunes of Iranian football.

MANAGER

TOMISLAV IVIC

PROFILE

A Croatian who has set his stall with a tough schedule for Iran after watching tapes of the qualifying games. Appointed in January 1998, 64-year-old Ivic was a player with Hajduk Split and at the end of his playing days started coaching, having worked in Belgium, Turkey, Italy, Greece, Portugal, Spain and France. After being put in charge of Iran, he ordered back-to-back training sessions and started to plan an 11-match build up to the World Cup finals.

KEY PLAYERS

ALI DAEI

Age: 29 **Club:** Arminia Bielefeld (Germany)

▶ Daei set up an internet site to petition his return to the national team after he was dropped as punishment.

▶ In 1996 he scored 22 international goals.

▶ He was picked last year for the Asian Select XI.

KARIM BAGHERI

Age: 24 **Club:** Arminia Bielefeld (Germany)

▶ He scored 17 goals in the World Cup qualifying rounds.

▶ He struck five times in Iran's 17-0 win over the Maldives.

▶ He plays in the German Bundesliga.

KHODADAD AZIZI

Age: 25 **Club:** FC Cologne (Germany)

▶ He scored the crucial equalizer against Australia in front of 120,000 fans in Tehran.

▶ He plays in the German Bundesliga, but turned down Borussia Dortmund because of the competition for places.

▶ He was voted Asian Footballer of the Year in 1997.

GROUP F

USA

ROAD TO FRANCE

Jamaica 0 USA 0 (2 March 1997)	USA 3 Canada 0 (16 March 1997)
Costa Rica 3 USA 2 (23 March 1997)	USA 2 Mexico 2 (20 April 1997)
El Salvador 1 USA 1 (29 June 1997)	USA 1 Costa Rica 0 (7 September 1997)
USA 1 Jamaica 1 (3 October 1997)	Mexico 0 USA 0 (2 November 1997)
Canada 0 USA 3 (9 November 1997)	USA 4 El Salvador 2 (16 November 1997)

WORLD CUP RECORD

The progress of football in America can be measured by their appearances in World Cup finals – and France '98 will be their third successive tournament. In 1994 they qualified as hosts, but they then surpassed all expectations by reaching the last 16 where eventual champions Brazil could only beat them 1-0. Their finest 90 minutes, however, came in 1950 when they beat England 1-0 in the Brazil finals. The USA did reach the semi-finals of the 1930 inaugural tournament, where they were thrashed 6-1 by Argentina, but then the invitation-only event was hardly representative of world football. Today, American footballers are emerging to play in other countries and from the 1994 experience, the likes of Alexi Lalas ended up in Italy, and Cobi Jones in the Premiership along with goalkeeper Kasey Keller.

KEY PLAYERS

KASEY KELLER Age: 28 Club: Leicester City (England)

▶ Keller captained 1996 US Olympic team and was runner-up in the 1997 US Player of the Year awards.
▶ He obtained a sociology degree by correspondence course after leaving Portland University to join Millwall in February 1992.
▶ He won a Coca-Cola Cup winner's medal as keeper for Leicester against Middlesbrough in April 1997.

MANAGER

PROFILE

STEVE SAMPSON

Steve Sampson made his mark coaching in American University football, leading Santa Clara in California to the college title. From there he progressed to the US national side and was an assistant to Bora Milutinovic in the USA's 1994 World Cup campaign. Sampson was promoted after Bora moved south to take charge of Mexico for a second time.

JOVAN KIROVSKI Age: 20 Club: Borussia Dortmund (Germany)

▶ Kirovski was born in Macedonia but brought up in San Diego.
▶ Spotted by Manchester United when on a youth tour, he emigrated to England, scored more than a goal a game in the Old Trafford youth team and was top scorer with 20 goals as the reserves won the 1995–96 Pontins League.
▶ He was refused a British work permit and now plays in Germany.

PREDRAG RADOSAVLJEVOIC Age: 34 Club: Kansas City Wiz

▶ He scored 399 goals in 370 games over nine years in US Indoor soccer.
▶ He had spells at Everton and Portsmouth before returning to the US and becoming Kansas captain.
▶ Known as 'Preki', he was born in Belgrade and represented Yugoslavia before emigrating to the United States, for whom he scored in the 4-2 final qualifying win over El Salvador.

GROUP F

Yugoslavia

ROAD TO FRANCE

Yugoslavia 3 Faroe Islands 1 (24 April 1996) | Yugoslavia 6 Malta 0 (2 June 1996)
Faroe Islands 1 Yugoslavia 8 (6 October 1996) | Yugoslavia 1 Czech Republic 0 (10 November 1996)
Spain 2 Yugoslavia 0 (14 December 1996) | Czech Republic 1 Yugoslavia 2 (2 April 1997)
Yugoslavia 1 Spain 1 (30 April 1997) | Yugoslavia 2 Slovakia 0 (8 June 1997)
Slovakia 1 Yugoslavgia 1 (10 September 1997) | Malta 0 Yugoslavia 5 (11 October 1997)
PLAY-OFF
Hungary 1 Yugoslavia 7 (29 October 1997) | Yugoslavia 5 Hungary 0 (15 November 1997)

WORLD CUP RECORD

This will be only the fourth World Cup finals that Yugoslavia have played since 1974, although they did leave an impressive mark on Italia '90. In Italy they reached the quarter-finals where they lost to Argentina on penalties. The quarter-finals – also reached in 1958 – are not unfamiliar territory to Yugoslavia, who enjoyed their best competition in Chile in 1962. That year they recovered from a 2-0 group-stage defeat by the USSR, to sweep past West Germany 1-0 in the last eight before going down 3-1 to Czechoslovakia in the semis. They had reached the semi-finals of the first competition in 1930, but were thrashed 6-1 by eventual winners Uruguay. There was a gap of 12 years from the Chile tournament to Yugoslavia's next appearance in Germany, where the first round group stage was negotiated in some style – a 0-0 draw with Brazil, a 9-0 thrashing of Zaire and a 1-1 draw with Scotland. Then the wheels came off as in the next group stage Yugoslavia lost to West Germany, Poland and Sweden. The trip to Spain in 1982 was brought to a premature halt by the hosts.

MANAGER *SLOBODAN SANTRAC*
PROFILE Slobodan Santrac was a former player with OFK Belgrade and then in Switzerland with Grasshopper Zurich, Santrac won eight caps for Yugoslavia. He was put in charge of the national team in 1994 and his success in guiding them to France '98 was made sweeter by the emphatic way they came through the play-off with Hungary, winning 12-1 on aggregate.

KEY PLAYERS

PREDRAG MIJATOVIC Age: 29
Club: Real Madrid (Spain)
▶ He scored 14 goals in the World Cup qualifying matches.
▶ In the 1995–96 season he scored 28 goals for Valencia.
▶ Real Madrid paid £6.3 million for him in 1996.

VLADIMIR JUGOVIC Age: 28 Club: Lazio (Italy)
▶ Has won the European Champions' Cup with Red Star Belgrade (1991) and Juventus (1996).
▶ He has one of the most powerful shots from open or set play in the game.
▶ He has now played for three top Italian teams: Sampdoria, Juventus and Lazio.

DEJAN SAVICEVIC Age: 31 Club: AC Milan (Italy)
▶ He has won more caps than any of the other squad members, with the exception of Dragan Stojkovic.
▶ Savicevic has played nearly 100 games for Milan, scored 20 times and set up countless other goals.
▶ He scored in Milan's 4-0 victory over Barcelona in the 1994 European Cup Final.

GROUP F

Germany

ROAD TO FRANCE

Armenia 1 Germany 5 (9 October 1996)	Ukraine 0 Germany 0 (7 June 1997)
Germany 1 Northern Ireland 1 (9 November 1996)	Northern Ireland 1 Germany 3 (20 August 1997)
Portugal 0 Germany 0 (14 December 1996)	Germany 1 Portugal 1 (6 September 1997)
Albania 2 Germany 3 (2 April 1997)	Germany 4 Armenia 0 (11 September 1997)
Germany 2 Ukraine 0 (30 April 1997)	Germany 4 Albania 3 (11 October 1997)

WORLD CUP RECORD

Only Brazil have won the competition more times than Germany, who have only missed the 1930 and 1950 World Cup finals.

The Germans won their first World Cup in 1954, upsetting the odds to triumph in Switzerland. In the Final against Hungary, the Germans were 2-0 down after eight minutes, but they would not give up and came back to win 3-2. They lost to England in the 1966 Final; won on home soil in 1974 when they beat Holland 2-1 after conceding a goal in the first minute; lost 3-1 to Italy in the Spanish World Cup of 1982; and four years later in Mexico went down 3-2 to Argentina.

They gained sweet revenge in 1990 when Andreas Brehme's penalty settled a dire Final in Italy where Germany won 1-0.

Defending their title in America, Germany reached the quarter-finals but were surprisingly knocked out by Bulgaria. As well as their past World Cup successes, Germany are also the holders of the European Championship – another trophy they have won three times.

MANAGER *BERTI VOGTS*

PROFILE

The name of Berti Vogts is familiar and so it should be. Vogts was a playing legend for Germany – 96 caps, a World Cup winner's medal in 1974 plus considerable club success with Monchengladbach, including two UEFA Cups. He has done his time coaching, having been at the helm of the Youth and Under-20 teams before joining Franz Beckenbauer in preparing the 1990 World Cup-winning national side. Vogts then took charge, but his team were surprisingly beaten in America by Bulgaria. The coach, however, has since made amends with success in the 1996 European Championship, won in sudden-death overtime against the Czech Republic.

KEY PLAYERS

CHRISTIAN ZIEGE Age: 26 Club: AC Milan (Italy)

- Left-back Ziege, who began his career as a goalkeeper, has often been compared to international legend Andreas Brehme.
- He made his international debut against Brazil at the US Cup in 1993 and has been a regular in the German side ever since.
- His greatest achievement at club level was his part in Bayern Munich's victory in the 1996 UEFA Cup.

JURGEN KOHLER

Age: 32 Club: Borussia Dortmund

- One of the game's most respected defenders, Kohler is known as 'Ironfoot' in his native Germany.
- His involvement in Euro '96 was ended prematurely when he injured knee ligaments in Germany's first game of the tournament.
- Kohler actually retired from international football after Euro '96 but was persuaded to reconsider after leading Borussia to a 3-1 European Cup triumph over former club Juventus in 1997.

JURGEN KLINSMANN

Age: 33 Club: Tottenham (England)

- Klinsmann succeeded Lothar Matthaus as German captain for Euro '96 and led his side to victory in the Final against the Czech Republic, despite tearing a calf muscle earlier in the tournament.
- Klinsmann has already confirmed he will retire from international football after the World Cup.
- In his first season with Tottenham Hotspur, Klinsmann finished as the club's leading scorer and was voted Footballer of the Year.

GROUP G

Tunisia

ROAD TO FRANCE

Rwanda 1 Tunisia 2 (2 June 1996)
Libria 0 Tunisia 1 (11 November 1996)
Namibia 1 Tunisia 2 (5 April 1997)
Egypt 0 Tunisia 0 (8 June 1997)

Tunisia 2 Rwanda 0 (16 June 1996)
Tunisia 1 Egypt 0 (12 January 1997)
Tunisia 2 Liberia 0 (27 April 1997)
Tunisia 4 Namibia 0 (17 August 1997)

WORLD CUP RECORD

The North African country have made just one visit to the World Cup finals – back in Argentina in 1978, and they made a flying start. A 3-1 win over Mexico made them the group's leading side, following a 0-0 draw between the other two teams, West Germany and Poland. Beaten 1-0 by Poland, Tunisia got up off the floor to draw 0-0 with West Germany, the defending World Champions. However, their results – a win, a draw and a defeat – were not quite good enough to take them through because of Germany's 6-0 demolition of Mexico. After that Tunisian football took a back seat until 1996 when a successful World Cup qualifying campaign went hand in hand with a successful run in the African Nations Cup. They reached the Final where they lost 2-0 to South Africa.

MANAGER PROFILE — *HENRYK KASPERCZAK*

Tunisians with a long memory might recall that their current coach Henryk Kasperczak was in the Poland team that beat them back in the World Cup finals of 1978. Kasperczak was a regular with Poland, playing in two World Cups, while his club football was with Metz in France. He later coached them to the French Cup before having spells with a number of other French clubs, among them Saint-Etienne, Strasbourg, Matra Racing, Montpellier and Lille. A five-month stint with the Ivory Coast – he took them to the semi-finals of the 1994 African Nations Cup – brought him to the attention of the Tunisian soccer authorities, who appointed him at the beginning of June 1994.

KEY PLAYERS

MEHDI BEN SLIMANE Age: 24 Club: Freiburg (Germany)

- Ben Slimane was playing with AS Marsa in Tunisia when he went to the African Nations Cup, but when Tunisia reached the Final he was snapped up by Marseille.
- The weighty winger is nicknamed 'Dicker' at the German club Freiburg, where he moved in 1996.
- He scored once in the World Cup qualifying campaign, against Rwanda.

ADEL SELLIMI
Age: 25 Club: Nantes (France)
- He is Tunisia's most capped player, having made over 50 appearances for his national side.
- The left-sided attacker was Tunisia's leading scorer in World Cup qualification, with four goals.
- While with Club Africain in Tunisia, he won three Championships, one Turkish Cup and the African Club Cup in 1991.

ZOUBIER BEYA
Age: 27 Club: Freiburg (Germany)
- The explosive midfielder joined his international team-mate Ben Slimane in Germany last season, leaving Tunisian club Etoile Sahel.
- He scored three goals on the road to France, including the only goal in the crunch match with Egypt.
- Beya, nicknamed 'Zouba' by the German fans, was one of the players of the tournament when Tunisia reached the Final of the 1996 African Nations Cup.

GROUP G

Romania

ROAD TO FRANCE

Romania 3 Lithuania 0 (31 August 1996) **Iceland 0 Romania 4** (19 October 1996)
Macedonia 0 Romania 3 (14 December 1996) **Romania 8 Liechtenstein 0** (29 March 1997)
Lithuania 0 Romania 1 (2 April 1997) **Romania 1 Ireland 0** (20 April 1997)
Romania 4 Macedonia 2 (20 August 1997) **Liechtenstein 1 Romania 8** (6 September 1997)
Romania 4 Iceland 0 (10 September 1997) **Ireland 1 Romania 1** (11 October 1997)

WORLD CUP RECORD

There was sweet revenge for Romania when they beat the Republic of Ireland at home and then, already qualified for France '98, held the Irish to a draw in the return fixture. This was the only point dropped by Romania in their qualifying campaign, and they are making their seventh appearance in the World Cup finals. Invited to take part in the first World Cup back in 1930 and appearing again in 1934 and 1938, Romania's best days have come in the 1990s. In Italia '90 they reached the last 16 where they were beaten 5-4 on penalties by the Republic of Ireland, and then in the USA four years ago they went one round better. Once again, however, they were undone by their failure in the penalty shoot-out. This time they drew 2-2 with Sweden in normal time and lost the shoot-out 5-4.

MANAGER PROFILE

VICTOR PITURCA

The former Romanian Under-21 coach took charge in March when Iordanescu was relieved of his duties. Like his predecessor, Piturca was a player with Steaua Bucharest and has some act to follow after Iordanescu led Romania to their best ever finish in the finals in 1994. The qualifying route for France '98 was also a triumph with 37 goals scored and just 4 conceded. Piturca, who was jailed under the communist regime of Romania, for gambling, was only released on the intervention of the former dictator Ceausescu.

KEY PLAYERS

BOGDAN STELEA

Age: 30 **Club:** Steaua Bucharest

▶ This goalkeeper is the David James of Romania – making blinding saves one moment, dropping clangers the next.

▶ He saved a penalty from Roy Keane in a key qualifying game against the Republic of Ireland. He had needlessly conceded the spot-kick by bringing down Ray Houghton.

▶ He has earned a living in five countries: Romania (Dinamo, Steaua Bucharest); Spain (Mallorca); Belgium (Standard Liege); Austria (Rapid Vienna); and Turkey (Samsunspor).

GHEORGHE HAGI

Age: 32 **Club:** Galatasaray (Turkey)

▶ His incredible skills have earned him the nickname 'Maradona of the Carpathians'.

▶ Current Republic of Ireland manager Mick McCarthy swapped shirts with Hagi after they faced each other in Italia '90. 'He's the best I've played against – I couldn't get near him,' said McCarthy.

▶ He won more free-kicks than any other player in both the 1990 and 1994 World Cups and will retire from international football after France '98.

DAN PETRESCU **Age:** 29 **Club:** Chelsea (England)

▶ His hardest opponent was Ruud Gullit, later his manager at Chelsea. They clashed when Petrescu played for Foggia and Genoa in Serie A and Gullit was the star of AC Milan.

▶ Petrescu won four championships in Romania with Steaua Bucharest – who reached the 1989 European Cup Final, losing 4-0 to AC Milan.

▶ He is the embodiment of the 1990s wing-back; technically excellent moving forward but also able to defend. It was England coach Glenn Hoddle who first put Petrescu in that role.

GROUP G

England

ROAD TO FRANCE

Moldova 0 England 3 (1 September 1996)	England 2 Georgia 0 (30 April 1997)
England 2 Poland 1 (9 October 1996)	Poland 0 England 2 (31 May 1997)
Georgia 0 England 2 (9 November 1996)	England 4 Moldova 0 (10 September 1997)
England 0 Italy 1 (12 February 1997)	Italy 0 England 0 (11 October 1997)

WORLD CUP RECORD

The glory year was 1966 – Geoff Hurst scoring the only hat-trick in a Final as England beat Germany 4-2 at Wembley in extra-time. Since then it has been a roller-coaster ride, with qualification failures punctuated by glimpses of success. In 1990 England came through the group stages to beat Belgium 1-0 with the last kick of the match. Next, Cameroon were beaten 3-2 in the quarter-final, again after extra-time, before a 1-1 draw in the semi-final against West Germany led to penalties and England losing 4-3. In 1986 they reached the quarter-finals where Argentina won 2-1 thanks to the infamous 'Hand of God' goal by Maradona.

In the 1990s England have rediscovered their form, reaching the semi-final of Euro '96 and winning a four-way tournament in France which also included Brazil and Italy. England did not play in their first World Cup finals until 1950 – when they were sensationally beaten by the USA. Four years later in Switzerland they reached the quarter-finals and were to do the same again in Chile in 1962. Failure to hang on to their trophy in 1970 led to a dark period when they failed to qualify for successive finals, in Germany and Argentina.

MANAGER GLENN HODDLE

PROFILE Glenn Hoddle was appointed when Terry Venables announced he was standing down in 1996. Hoddle has made his mark on the team and moulded them in his playing image – gifted and full of passing movement. A stalwart with Tottenham and then Monaco, he moved into coaching with Swindon Town and was then snapped up by Chelsea. He made a considerable impression at the London club, and once Venables announced he was leaving the England job, Hoddle became the only acceptable candidate for his replacement.

KEY PLAYERS

ALAN SHEARER
Age: 27 **Club:** Newcastle United

◗ Shearer became the most expensive player in the world when he joined Newcastle from Blackburn Rovers for £15 million in July 1996.
◗ He finished Euro '96 as the tournament's leading scorer with five goals from five appearances.
◗ He was the Premiership's leading scorer for three consecutive seasons between 1994–95 and 1996–97, but missed most of the 1997–98 season with a serious ankle injury.

DAVID SEAMAN **Age:** 34 **Club:** Arsenal

◗ Seaman has been England's first-choice goalkeeper for the past four seasons.

◗ He was instrumental in England's progress to the semi-finals of Euro '96, saving a penalty in the group stages against Scotland and another in the quarter-final penalty shoot-out against Spain.
◗ He has won every English domestic trophy in his 12 years with Arsenal and also has a 1994 European Cup Winners' Cup medal.

DAVID BECKHAM
Age: 23 **Club:** Manchester United

◗ Beckham is famous for his long-range shooting and scored a spectacular goal from the half-way line on the opening day of the 1996–97 season against Wimbledon.
◗ He was voted the PFA Young Player of the Year in 1996–97
◗ Beckham has attracted a lot of attention because of his engagment to Spice Girl Victoria Adams.

GROUP G

Colombia

ROAD TO FRANCE

Colombia 1 Paraguay 0 (24 April 1996)	Paraguay 2 Colombia 1 (2 April 1997)
Peru 1 Colombia 1 (2 June 1996)	Colombia 0 Peru 1 (30 April 1997)
Colombia 3 Uruguay 1 (7 July 1996)	Uruguay 1 Colombia 1 (8 June 1997)
Colombia 4 Chile 1 (1 September 1996)	Chile 4 Colombia 1 (5 July 1997)
Ecuador 0 Colombia 1 (9 October 1996)	Colombia 1 Ecuador 0 (20 July 1997)
Bolivia 2 Colombia 2 (10 November 1996)	Colombia 3 Bolivia 0 (20 August 1997)
Venezuela 0 Colombia 2 (15 November 1996)	Colombia 1 Venezuela 0 (27 September 1997)
Colombia 0 Argentina 1 (12 February 1997)	Argentina 1 Colombia 1 (16 November 1997)

WORLD CUP RECORD

Colombia have reached three World Cup finals, but 1990 was the first tournament that saw them progress beyond the first stage. Their first appearance was in 1962 in Chile, where they lost in the group stage to Yugoslavia and Uruguay, but managed an entertaining 4-4 draw with the USSR. In 1990 a 2-0 win over the United Arab Emirates and a draw with Germany was enough to take them through to uncharted waters – the last 16. There they faced another side new to this level of football – Cameroon. In the end Colombia were beaten 2-1 in extra-time. In 1994, having arrived in America as strongly tipped outsiders, they came apart at the seams. They were beaten 3-1 by Romania and 2-1 by the USA, before salvaging some pride with a 2-0 win over Switzerland. Many wondered how a country with such fabulous extrovert talents as Faustino Asprilla, Freddy Rincon, goalkeeper Rene Higuita and Carlos Valderrama could lose the plot so badly. There was talk of betting coups and the subsequent murder of defender Andres Escobar – the man who scored a disastrous own goal in the match with the USA – added to the rumours.

MANAGER PROFILE

HERNAN DARIO GOMEZ

Hernan Dario Gomez was appointed after the 1994 World Cup. He played in Medellin, first with Independiente and then Atletico before becoming the coach to the Colombia Olympic team in 1993. Following this, he became the right-hand man to Francisco Maturana for the USA trip in 1994. The failure of the Colombians saw more change and Gomez promoted. He managed to bring his side through a long qualifying section and inspired them to pick up their game after a run of three defeats in February and April 1997 – by Argentina, Paraguay and Peru – which threatened to derail their drive for France.

KEY PLAYERS

FAUSTINO ASPRILLA

Age: 29 **Club:** Parma (Italy)

▶ Signed by Kevin Keegan for £7.5 million, Asprilla remained at St James' Park for a further year under Dalglish before moving to Italy.

▶ His most impressive performance for Newcastle was the hat-trick he scored in the 3-2 win over Barcelona.

▶ He was Colombia's top scorer in the qualification matches, hitting the target seven times, including a hat-trick against Chile.

FREDDY RINCON

Age: 31 **Club:** Corinthians of Sao Paulo (Brazil)

▶ Rincon is a veteran on the World Cup stage, having played for Colombia in both Italia '90 and USA '94.

▶ He has previously had spells in both Italy (Napoli) and Spain (Real Madrid), but prefers football in Brazil: 'You can enjoy yourself more on the field.'

▶ In Italia '90, he saved Colombia from elimination when he scored a late equalizing goal against Germany, finishing a stunning series of passes which had completely split the German team.

CARLOS VALDERRAMA

Age: 36 **Club:** Tampa Bay (USA)

▶ Another Colombian veteran, he won his 100th cap in August 1997 against Jamaica.

▶ He is famous for his bizarre hairstyle, a cascading blonde afro.

▶ He has twice been voted South American Player of the Year.

GROUP H

Japan

ROAD TO FRANCE

Japan 6 Uzbekistan 3 (6 September 1997) **UAE 0 Japan 0** (12 September 1997)
Japan 1 South Korea 2 (28 September 1997) **Kazakhstan 1 Japan 1** (4 October 1997)
Uzbekistan 1 Japan 1 (11 October 1997)   **Japan 1 UAE 1** (26 October 1997)
South Korea 0 Japan 2 (1 November 1997) **Japan 5 Kazakhstan 1** (8 November 1997)
PLAY-OFF
Japan 3 Iran 2 (16 November 1997)

WORLD CUP RECORD

The Japanese have never played in the World Cup finals before, but their love of football cannot be denied. They have a thriving League system and money to support it – after all, Grampus 8 were the Japanese club with the financial clout to sign Gary Lineker when he wound down his career away from England. Japan won the 1992 Asian Cup, staged in Hiroshima, and a willingness to organize and house whatever tournaments are going, along with a restructuring of the leagues, has helped develop the game. So successful were Japan in hosting the World Club Championship back in 1980 that the annual match between Europe's best club side and South America's club kings has not been held anywhere else since. Japan's biggest step in giving football prominence will come in four years' time when they are the joint-hosts of the 2002 World Cup with South Korea. Japan is ready for top-class football.

MANAGER / PROFILE — *TAKESHI OKADA*

Takeshi Okada was appointed in October 1996, replacing Shu Kamo as the national team manager, and he was able to give the country the lift needed to qualify for the World Cup finals. In his early forties, Okada has changed the pattern of play; his Japan are a fast-moving attacking side and, having qualified via a play-off, will be eager to show the world that they are not just in France to make up the numbers.

KEY PLAYERS

KAZU MIURA Age: 30 Club: Verdy Kawasaki
▶ Miura played a season in Italy in 1994–95, taking a £1 million pay cut to join Genoa – just to add European football to his CV.
▶ He left Japan at the age of 15 to go to Brazil, the home of his hero Pelé, and was offered a professional contract with Santos.
▶ The pin-up of Japanese soccer scored 14 goals in the World Cup qualifying campaign – including two hat-tricks against Macao and one against Uzbekistan.

YOSIKATSU KAWAGUCHI
Age: 21 Club: Yokohama Marinos
▶ The Japanese No. 1 goalkeeper saved over 30 shots from the Brazilian team when they played in the 1996 Olympics.
▶ He learned his trade at the centre of Japanese school football, Shimizu Commercial Senior High, and then had offers from seven clubs.
▶ In 1995 he was voted the Japanese League's Rookie of the Year, after keeping five clean sheets in his first five League games.

HIDETOSHI NAKATA Age: 21 Club: Bellmare Hiratsuka
▶ Nakata has said that he would prefer book tokens to medals as prizes for winning football honours.
▶ He won an Asian Cup-Winners' Cup medal with Bellmare Hiratsuka in 1995.
▶ He had a spell training in Italy and wants to play abroad, seeing the World Cup as an opportunity to impress.

GROUP H

Croatia

ROAD TO FRANCE

Bosnia 1 Croatia 4 (9 October 1996)
Croatia 1 Denmark 1 (29 March 1997)
Greece 0 Croatia 1 (30 April 1997)
Denmark 3 Croatia 1 (10 September 1997)
PLAY-OFF
Croatia 2 Ukraine 0 (29 October 1997)

Croatia 1 Greece 1 (10 November 1996)
Croatia 3 Slovenia 3 (2 April 1997)
Croatia 3 Bosnia 2 (6 September 1997)
Slovenia 1 Croatia 3 (11 October 1997)

Ukraine 1 Croatia 1 (11 November 1997)

WORLD CUP RECORD

A state that only became a country in 1992 and was the focus for violent Balkan unrest, Croatia and Croatians see the football team as a means of bringing a united purpose to a newly-recognized country. The after-math led to 1,500 players leaving the country and reduced Croatian football to two professional clubs: Hadjuk Split and Croatia Zagreb. As a consequence, it has been difficult to sustain interest in local football, not just with the fans but with the players. Many have left to try their hand in other countries – among them Aljosa Asanovic, who spent some time at Derby County and is now at Benefica in Portugal, and Slaven Bilic who went to Everton via West Ham. Croatia's first major competition was Euro '96 in England.

MANAGER *MIROSLAV BLAZEVIC*

PROFILE

Miroslav Blazevic is nicknamed 'Attila' because of his short temper. Blazevic has marched around Europe gaining experience and saving money. He first worked as a coach in Switzerland, moved to Nantes in France before going to Greece, then returning to Croatia in 1993. The homecoming was to buy Croatia Zagreb – the club formerly known as HASK Gradjanski and then Dinamo Zagreb. He was appointed national team coach in place of Vlatko Markovic in March 1994.

KEY PLAYERS

DAVOR SUKER
Age: 30 **Club:** Real Madrid (Spain)

◗ Suker scored one of the most memorable goals of Euro '96 when he lobbed Denmark's Peter Schmeichel from an acute angle on the edge of the penalty area.
◗ He was top scorer for the Yugoslavia side which lifted the 1987 World Youth Cup.
◗ Suker's international record of nearly a goal a game is much better than his scoring rate in club football.

ALEN BOKSIC **Age:** 28 **Club:** Lazio (Italy)

◗ Boksic won the European Cup during his spell with Marseille in France in 1993, but narrowly failed to repeat the feat when his Juventus side lost the 1997 Final to Borussia Dortmund.
◗ He is currently in his second spell with Lazio, after originally joining them for £8 million.
◗ He was a member of Yugoslavia's World Cup squad at the 1990 finals in Italy, but did not play.

ROBERT PROSINECKI **Age:** 29 **Club:** Croatia Zagreb

◗ Prosinecki's pinpoint passing was a key feature in Red Star Belgrade's European Cup winning side in 1991.
◗ Now with Croatia Zagreb, the club which rejected him as a youngster, Prosinecki has played for both of Spain's premier clubs – Real Madrid and Barcelona.
◗ He won 15 caps for Yugoslavia and represented the country in the 1990 World Cup in Italy.

GROUP H

Argentina

ROAD TO FRANCE

Argentina 3 Bolivia 1 (24 April 1996)	Colombia 0 Argentina (12 February 1997)
Ecuador 2 Argentina 0 (2 June 1996)	Bolivia 2 Argentina 1 (2 April 1997)
Peru 0 Argentina 0 (7 July 1996)	Argentina 2 Ecuador 1 (30 April 1997)
Argentina 1 Paraguay 1 (1 September 1996)	Argentina 2 Peru 0 (7 June 1997)
Venezuela 2 Argentina 5 (9 October 1996)	Paraguay 1 Argentina 2 (6 July 1997)
Argentina 1 Chile 1 (15 December 1996)	Argentina 2 Venezuela 0 (20 July 1997)
Uruguay 0 Argentina 0 (12 January 1997)	Chile 1 Argentina 2 (10 September 1997)
Argentina 0 Uruguay 0 (12 October 1997)	Argentina 1 Colombia 1 (16 November 1997)

WORLD CUP RECORD

One of the great nations in the history of the World Cup, Argentina were there at the very beginning and were the first finalists, losing 4-2 to Uruguay. In 1958 they were beaten 6-1 in the group stage by Czechoslovakia and 3-1 by West Germany, but they fared slightly better in 1966 when they reached the quarter-final, only to lose 1-0 in a bad-tempered match with the eventual winners, England. By 1974 Argentina were developing, but the breakthrough was to come on home soil in 1978 when, inspired by Mario Kempes and current manager Daniel Passarella, they came through the first round as group runners-up but in the second group stage beat Poland 2-0, drew 0-0 with Brazil and then thrashed Peru 6-0. Facing Holland in the Final, Argentina won 3-1 in extra time, Kempes scoring twice.

A determined defence of their title ended at the second stage in Spain 1982, but they were back in force in 1986, with Maradona as the key figure. His controversial 'Hand of God' winner, which beat England 2-1 in the quarter-final, was followed by a 2-0 victory over Belgium to set up a Final with Germany which Argentina won 3-2. The defending champions made a dismal start in 1990, but soon regained their form to face Germany in the Final. Here, they gave the appearance of wanting to win the Cup by hanging on for yet another penalty shoot-out but were undone by a penalty conceded in the normal course of play. In America in 1994 they reached the last 16 but were knocked out 3-2 by Romania.

KEY PLAYERS

ARIEL ORTEGA   Age: 24 Club: Valencia (Spain)

◆ Ortega is considered by many to be the best Argentinian player since Diego Maradona.

◆ Although only 23, he has already made over 30 appearances for his country and was practically an ever-present in the qualifying games for France '98.

◆ His £7 million transfer from River Plate was an Argentinian record.

GABRIEL BATISTUTA   Age: 29

Club: Fiorentina (Italy)

◆ Batistuta was short-listed for European Footballer of the Year in 1997.

◆ He is a veteran at international level, having played over 50 games for Argentina, including the 1994 World Cup campaign.

◆ He joined Fiorentina in 1991 and, although the team got relegated from Serie A the following season, he stayed with them and helped them earn promotion. He has vowed to end his playing days at the club.

JAVIER ZANETTI   Age: 23

Club: Inter Milan (Italy)

◆ Zanetti is a firm favourite with the Inter Milan fans for his tenacious work-rate and remarkably consistent performances.

◆ As a teenager, he was put a diet of beans, lentils and milk because he was so small and light. It worked.

◆ He was a member of Argentina's silver medal-winning team at the 1996 Atlanta Olympics.

MANAGER	*DANIEL PASSARELLA*
PROFILE	Daniel Passarella is one of the privileged few to have been summoned forward to collect the World Cup, having led Argentina to victory in 1978. Passarella became a giant of the game, a star in his home country with River Plate and then

in Italy at Inter Milan and Fiorentina. Now in his mid-forties, he was appointed team coach in 1994 and guided his country through a long qualifying process, stabilizing the team after early disappointments including a 2-0 defeat by Ecuador and draws with Peru and Paraguay.

GROUP H

Jamaica

ROAD TO FRANCE

Jamaica 0 USA 0 (2 March 1997)	Mexico 6 Jamaica 0 (13 April 1997)
Canada 0 Jamaica 0 (29 April 1997)	Costa Rica 3 Jamaica 1 (11 May 1997)
Jamaica 1 El Salvador 0 (18 May 1997)	Jamaica 1 Canada 0 (7 September 1997)
Jamaica 1 Costa Rica 0 (14 September 1997)	USA 1 Jamaica 1 (3 October 1997)
El Salvador 2 Jamaica 2 (9 November 1997)	Jamaica 0 Mexico 0 (16 November 1997)

WORLD CUP RECORDS

Debutants in the World Cup, France '98 will be a huge adventure for Jamaica – a country which, when the qualifying process started, could never have dreamed of making it to the finals. They had to play ten pre-qualifying matches to reach the CONCACAF final group where one goal scored, two draws and two defeats – including a 6-0 thrashing by Mexico – did not augur well. But from then on in, Jamaica were unbeaten and they clinched their place with a creditable draw in the return with Mexico in their last qualifying match.

MANAGER PROFILE *RENE SIMOES*

Attack is the only way, and you would expect little else from a country coached by a Brazilian, Rene Simoes. He has turned the laid-back Reggae Boyz, as Jamaica are known, into a side full of exciting and unexpected football. Simoes has been in charge since 1994 and qualifying for France is a major achievement. No one would expect them to win, but Jamaica will enjoy the experience.

KEY PLAYERS

DEON BURTON

Age: 21 **Club:** Derby County (England)

▶ He made 62 appearances in four seasons for Portsmouth and cost Derby £1 million.
▶ Born in Reading, Berkshire, he qualifies for Jamaica because his father came from the island.
▶ He scored in his first four World Cup matches against Costa Rica, Canada, USA and El Salvador.

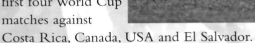

FITZROY SIMPSON **Age:** 28 **Club:** Portsmouth (England)

▶ Born in the English West Country market town of Trowbridge, he has a Jamaican father.
▶ He began as a left winger, but has operated efficiently at right-back for Portsmouth since the 1996–97 season.
▶ He started his career with local League club Swindon before moving to Manchester City for £500,000 in March 1992.

PAUL HALL **Age:** 25 **Club:** Portsmouth (England)

▶ Born in Manchester of a Jamaican father, he started his career with Torquay United.
▶ He paid his own air fare to attend trials for the Jamaican World Cup campaign.
▶ He partnered Deon Burton in a twin attack for Portsmouth but later moved back to operate just behind the front two.

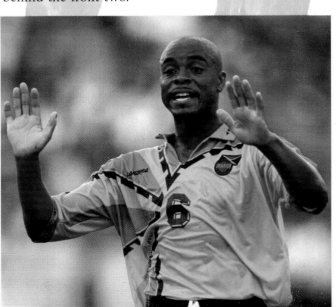

Crème de la Prem

From A to W, Arsenal to Wimbledon, the Premiership is a galaxy of world stars. England has become a centre for international football with the cream of international talent seduced by the challenge, the glamour and the tradition of the English game. Loads of money from Sky TV and a rumbling of real faith in the England team have helped to lift football to a higher plain. The 1990s has been a bull-market for football. England were expected to do well in Euro '96 and didn't do too badly, reaching the semi-finals where they were beaten in a penalty shoot-out by who else but Germany. Since then Glenn Hoddle has replaced Terry Venables as coach and the expectations for England have risen, built upon the evidence of the way England have qualified for France rather than blind faith.

All of this means that to keep up, even progress, in world football, the players of the world see England as the place to be – the fact that the money in the game now makes it a nice little earner is a sweetener, but far from the sole motivation.

It is no coincidence that Arsenal's Dennis Bergkamp, who first played for the club at the start of the 1995–96 season, has been playing the best football of his life. This is a man who has been with Ajax of Holland, and Inter Milan of Italy, but in England at Highbury he has been on top of his game like never before. That he has managed this in a league perceived abroad as one of high-speed football played over a gruelling period of time on pitches that turn into winter quagmires, has put paid to a myth or two. The fact is that the English game has probably made Bergkamp a better player too. There is no respite, no time to rest on his laurels, no break to reflect on the challenge ahead.

He has to get on with it. The truly great players will solve the problems of new challenges.

So while Holland will probably have an even sharper striker in France '98, how will England have benefited by providing regular work for the likes of Bergkamp? Simple – the job of containing him has made better players of those Englishmen who have had to deal with the problem.

Arsene Wenger, the French coach at Arsenal, has brought in a few of his countrymen, but his

biggest signing was another Dutchman, Marc Overmars, signed from Ajax for £7 million, and that corner of north London has become a little Holland. Down in the south west, Chelsea has become the little Italy. Gianluca Vialli, Gianfranco Zola and Roberto di Matteo have all migrated here.

All three have shone: di Matteo scoring a remarkable FA Cup Final goal for Chelsea in 1996, finding the net inside a minute; Vialli contributing goals and now coaching the side; and Zola becoming one of the most admired stars of the English game.

It was Zola who scored for Italy in a 1-0 win over England at Wembley in a World Cup qualifying game. The England team knew all about Zola, but even so were unable to contain the diminutive Italian. Zola is a natural, but has done more for English football than light up the game with his skills. His attitude and love of the game is so apparent that even England supporters – once the home nation had qualified for France '98 – could applaud and admire him week-in and week-out as he plays for Chelsea. Zola was the 1997 Footballer of the Year and emphatic proof that the quality players from around the world do make a contribution.

Chelsea, until recently coached by the former Dutch international Ruud Gullit, are as exotic a club as they come. For as well as the Italian contingent, they have the Romanian Dan Petrescu, France's Frank Leboeuf and the Norwegian striker Tore Andre Flo. It seems that no corner of the English game has been untouched by continental hands: Aston Villa have had Savo Milosevic on the books; Barnsley the Dutch defender Arjan De Zeeuw; while Bolton have two players from Denmark in Per Frandsen and Michael Johansen.

What is most surprising about the pulling-power of English football is the sort of clubs who are buying top international stars. The lure of Manchester United, Newcastle, Liverpool or Arsenal is obvious. They are world-famous; they play in European tournaments and they have histories littered with garlands of success. Any player would be at the very least interested in joining such a club – but what of some of the other sides?

Take Crystal Palace. A yo-yo side who have been in and out of the Premiership throughout the 1990s, their European club experience limited to the Anglo-Italian Cup of the late 1960s and early 1970s (they actually beat Inter Milan in Italy). Surviving in the Premiership in their first season back was the be-all and end-all of their ambitions – yet they signed Attilio Lombardo of Juventus and Italy.

Lombardo has done it all, seen it and won it. Yet Palace managed to tempt him to south London and found themselves with a player receptive to the club and its short-term restricted ambitions. Even more remarkable, Lombardo managed to maintain his place in the Italy squad. In his second game for the club, a 2-0 win at Leeds United, Lombardo was substituted towards the end of the match, having given a superb performance. The Leeds supporters, in an almost unheard-of gesture, rose to applaud him. Whatever the club, great talent is appreciated and the influx of foreigners to the English game has made football connoisseurs of even the most partisan of fans.

Derby have Costa Rican Paulo Wanchope who in the 1996–97 season inspired his club to a sensational 3-2 win at Old Trafford, one of only two defeats

United suffered on their own soil. Leicester have an American goalkeeper in Kasey Keller; and on and on it goes. Established European stars looking for the challenge provided by English football; would-be foreign players proving that they can cut it at the highest level.

What of Manchester United, Liverpool and Newcastle? United have prospered on the remarkable youth policy put in place by Alex Ferguson, but his eyes are not closed to the rest of the world: Peter Schmeichel, the goalkeeper and rock of the defence, came from Denmark and Brondby, while striker Ole Gunnar Solskjaer, a Norwegian, has settled comfortably. Sometimes a buy from abroad works, sometimes it doesn't. Jordi Cruyff joined United from Barcelona for the start of the 1996-97 season, but despite international honours, did not find it easy to win a place in the starting line-up.

Liverpool have looked to Scandinavian players with mixed results – Stig Bjornebye and Bjorn Kvarme from Norway, Oyvind Leonhardsen from the same country but via Wimbledon. In attack they have opted for Karlheinz Riedle, the German who won a European Cup medal with Borussia Dortmund. That sort of moment is enjoyed by so few players and can be used as an incentive and an example of what can be achieved. Players like Riedle also bring bags of experience to their new clubs.

Newcastle spread their net wider and had Faustino Asprilla in their side for a while; the Colombian bringing a touch that no British player has ever had. Closer to home, Philippe Albert, the Belgian, has been a huge success and rock solid in defence.

There is a down side to this rise in imports. It might reflect the financial health of top football in England, but it also points to a domestic transfer market that is asking too much for home-grown players. Foreigners provide cheaper alternatives, a touch of the unknown and, in more cases than not, a determination to do well in their new workplace.

The international tournaments – the European Championship and the World Cup – provide a showcase for talents and it hardly takes the magic of the crystal ball to predict that after France '98 there will be more foreigners in the Premiership. They will light up many a cold November Saturday afternoon with their skills and the baggage of memories they will bring from France; and with a competition that takes in 32 countries in the final stages, we can expect the net to be spread wider. After all, the 1994 World Cup in the USA brought the likes of Cobi Jones to Coventry City, and this time there are more players in the shop window.

The success of England in the World Cup will have a long-term effect on how attractive the Premiership appears to foreign players – but rest assured, the English top division had, and still has, a reputation for being the toughest in the world. In the last few years it has enhanced this reputation by becoming one of the best in terms of skill and excitement – players, whether reared at home or from abroad, will be desperate to play in it.

France could be just a staging post for England on the road to having the best football in the world – every weekend of the season.

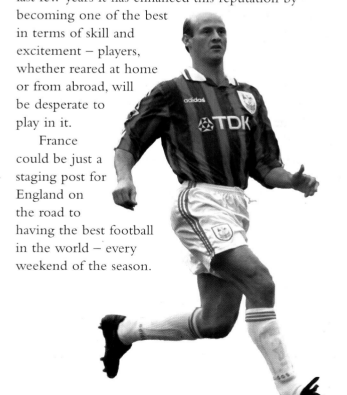

The Grounds

MARSEILLE

England kick off their campaign in the deep south of France against Tunisia in Marseille, the largest port on the Mediterranean. A city that is a cosmopolitan mix, both in appearance and inhabitants, Marseille is the cultural centre of southern France and boasts more theatres per capita than anywhere else in the country. In terms of appearance, industrial docks stand beside a city centre that is both ancient and picturesque, dating back 2,600 years. There should be no trouble finding your way around because signposts in six different languages have been installed.

The stadium: Stade Vélodrome.
The refurbished Vélodrome now has a 60,000 all-seated capacity and it is found right in the heart of the city. Home to Olympique Marseille, the locals are devoted football fans.

Getting there: Regular flights from England, five hours by train from Paris.
The matches: France v South Africa (12 June), *England* v Tunisia (15 June), Holland v South Korea (20 June), Brazil v Norway (23 June).

TOULOUSE

Just 60 miles from the Spanish border, with the Spanish influence strongly felt in the bars and restaurants, this is the fourth biggest city in France and a university town. Toulouse University was founded in 1229 and a quarter of the inhabitants are students. Its most striking feature is the pink brick buildings in the Capitole and Daurade areas. Toulouse is a strong rugby area.

The stadium: Stadium Municipal.
Oval-shaped and situated on an island between two branches of the River Garonne, the ground is still centrally located and has been refurbished. There were 34,000 places, many with a restricted view. Now there are 37,000 sheltered seats, all with a clear view. Ground shared by rugby and football teams.
Getting there: Regular flights from England, five trains a day from Paris – five hour journey.
The matches: Cameroon v Austria (11 June), Argentina v Japan (14 June), South Africa v Denmark (18 June), Romania v *England* (22 June), Nigeria v Paraguay (24 June).

LENS

The closest location to England, Lens, in the Nord Pas de Calais region, was a major battleground area on the Western Front in the Great War. Today, cemeteries remind visitors of the past. Until the 1960s it was a huge coal-mining area but recession saw the mines close and now new technology has made its mark. Lens is the smallest of the cities hosting World Cup matches, but has an enthusiastic following and a young audience – 41 per cent of the locals are under 25.
The stadium: Stade Félix Bollaert.
Renovated to become an all-seat stadium. The capacity has dropped from almost 52,000 to 41,275, but the tight ground – found 15 minutes away from the centre

The stadium: Stade de France.
A state of the art construction, the facilities are geared towards the comforts of spectators and players and it is a multi-purpose arena with a maximum audience capacity of 105,000. Surrounded by a running track, the design of the stands is such that the configuration can be made to suit the needs of the event being held.
Getting there: Regular flights to Paris, St Denis is on the airport side of the city. Also Eurostar.
The matches: Brazil v Scotland (10 June), Holland v Belguim (13 June), France v Saudi Arabia (18 June), Italy v Austria (23 June), Romania v Tunisia (26 June).

of Lens – is a favourite with French footballers because of its friendly atmosphere.
Getting there: Fly to Paris and then by train, one hour journey. Otherwise take Eurostar direct to Lille, the neighbouring city.
The matches: Saudi Arabia v Denmark (12 June), Jamaica v Croatia (14 June), Germany v Yugoslavia (21 June), Spain v Bulgaria (24 June), Colombia v *England* (26 June).

PARIS ST DENIS

Home for the World Cup Final, the purpose-built stadium cost £100 million and seats 80,000. Founded in a suburb of Paris, the high-tech facility has 50 bars on-site. An industrial location where Siemens and

Panasonic have bases, the World Cup has led to a considerable regeneration of the area. Named after Denis, the first bishop of Lutetia who, according to legend, was beheaded at Monmartre in the third century and walked to St Denis with his head under his arm.

BORDEAUX

Anyone who strolls round a supermarket will know Bordeaux is wine country – some 500 million bottles are produced here. In the region are the famous vineyards of Graves and Sauternes, Medoc, Pomerol and St Emillon. Described by Victor Hugo as 'Versailles with a pinch of Antwerp', Bordeaux was an outpost of the Roman Empire, although prosperity really arrived in the 18th century. The Garonne river flows through the sedate town which comes dramatically alive when the local football team is doing well.

The stadium: Parc de Lescure.
A national heritage monument, the Parc de Lescure was opened for a World Cup quarter-final match in 1938. There are 32,500 seats, of which only 15,000 are under cover, but the weather is normally good. Centrally located, it is just over a mile from the station and town centre.
Getting there: There is a local airport which takes direct flights from Gatwick, otherwise hourly trains run from Paris – the journey takes three hours.

The matches: Italy v Chile (11 June), Scotland v Norway (16 June), Belgium v Mexico (20 June), South Africa v Saudi Arabia (24 June), Argentina v Croatia (26 June).

LYON

The second-largest city in France, Lyon is a blend of the old (quaint cobbled streets) and the modern (the most impressive art gallery outside Paris). Famous for silk weaving, Lyon is the oldest archeological site outside Rome and was built on a hill by the Rhone river. It was here that the Lumière brothers first brought the cinema to life. Over four million tourists visit the area every year and the football ground hosted two matches in the 1997 Tournoi de France.

The stadium: Stade de Gerland.
Another ground listed as a historical monument. It was designed by Tony Garnier and draws on Roman architecture for its inspiration. There are four symbolic gateways to the grass-banked ground which, in a face-lift, has raised its capacity from 42,000 to 44,000 for the World Cup.

Getting there: Direct flights from the main airports in England. Trains hourly from Paris — journey time, two hours.
The matches: South Korea v Mexico (13 June), Romania v Colombia (15 June), USA v Iran (21 June), France v Denmark (24 June), Japan v Jamaica (26 June).

MONTPELLIER

The world's first medical school was founded in Montpellier, a city which has strong Spanish links and over the years has been at the heart of a religious struggle between Spanish Catholics and Protestants. A halt on the pilgrim road to Santiago de Compostela,

Montpellier is famed as a university city which has been attended at varying times by Nostradamus and Rabelais. Now much of the heart of the city is a traffic-free area and Montpellier has a growing place in the French economy. In two decades it has grown from the 21st largest city in the country to the eighth.

The stadium: La Mosson.
Only ten years old, considerable work has been done to improve the stadium which had a small capacity of 30,000, some of which was standing. It can now house 35,000, and there is a homely feel to the ground which can be found in a suburb out of the heart of the city. The improvements to the stadium have reflected the success of the home team.

Getting there: Direct flights or by train — there are five a day from Paris. The journey takes four and a half hours.
The matches: Morocco v Norway (10 June), Paraguay v Bulgaria (12 June), Italy v Cameroon (17 June), Colombia v Tunisia (22 June), Germany v Iran (25 June).

NANTES

A major port on the Atlantic Ocean, the landmark of Nantes is the castle that was once home to the Dukes of Nomandy. Today the city turns out 1,000 engineers every year and is a thriving research centre. Jules Verne was born in Nantes and the surreal art movement first started here. A famous cultural centre, Nantes has an opera house and runs two festivals, a carnival in the spring and a music festival in June. It is the capital of the Loire region. The football club, Nantes-Atlantique, have won the French championship seven times.

The stadium: Stade de la Beaujoire.
Built in 1984 to host some of the European Championship matches of that year, the 52,000 capacity — of which 17,000 was standing — has been dramati-

cally reduced to make for a 40,000 all-seat stadium. It is located about two miles out of the main city.

Getting there: No direct flights – but it can be reached by air travellers changing in Paris. Otherwise the train – a two-hour journey from the capital.

The matches: Spain v Nigeria (13 June), Brazil v Morocco (16 June), Japan v Croatia (20 June), Chile v Cameroon (23 June), USA v Yugoslavia (25 June)

ST ÉTIENNE

A coal-mining centre in the 19th century, St Étienne has had to reinvent itself to embrace new industries. It was also the centre of France's arms industry and a major manufacturing centre for bicycles. It is more famous, however, for its protected parkland outside the town. The town annually hosts an important book fair.

The stadium: Stade Geoffroy Guichard.
Renovated and down-sized to make it an all-seat stadium, the Geoffroy Guichard holds 36,000 spectators. Parking facilities have been increased and there is a new tree-lined access road to the ground.

Getting there: Flights from Britain to Lyon and then a 35-minute journey to St Étienne.

The matches: Yugoslavia v Iran (14 June), Chile v Austria (17 June), Spain v Paraguay (19 June), Scotland v Morocco (23 June), Holland v Mexico (25 June).

PARIS

The City of Light and one of the great capitals of the world, Paris has everything from the finest culture, the Louvre and the Mona Lisa, through to architectural wonders of the world: Notre Dame, the Eiffel Tower, Sacre Coeur. A vibrant night life to cater for all tastes with high-class opera, classical music, jazz, pop and the cabaret of the Moulin Rouge. Paris is also famous for its restaurants and shopping. Wide boulevards and an efficient underground train system make travelling around easy and Paris is a city always moving with the times.

The stadium: Parc des Princes.
Opened in 1972, Parc des Princes now takes second-place to the new St Denis stadium, but is still a vibrant arena for sport. The acoustics of the stadium make for a wall of sound that is so loud it will seem there are more than 49,000 people housed within the concrete structure.

Getting there: Regular flights from Britain and Eurostar to the centre of the city – just two hours from the English Channel.

The matches: Germany v USA (15 June), Nigeria v Bulgaria (19 June), Argentina v Jamaica (21 June), Belgium v South Korea (25 June).

Local kick-off times shown.

TOURNAMENT PLANNER FRANCE '98

	Team	Venue	Time		Winner	Score
A	BRAZIL v SCOTLAND	PARIS SF	10 JUNE 5.30			:
	MOROCCO v NORWAY	MONTPELLIER	10 JUNE 9.00			:
	NORWAY v SCOTLAND	BORDEAUX	16 JUNE 5.30			:
	BRAZIL v MOROCCO	NANTES	16 JUNE 9.00			:
	BRAZIL v NORWAY	MARSEILLE	23 JUNE 9.00			:
	MOROCCO v SCOTLAND	ST ÉTIENNE	23 JUNE 9.00			:
B	CHILE v ITALY	BORDEAUX	11 JUNE 5.30			:
	AUSTRIA v CAMEROON	TOULOUSE	11 JUNE 9.00			:
	AUSTRIA v CHILE	ST ÉTIENNE	17 JUNE 5.30			:
	CAMEROON v ITALY	MONTPELLIER	17 JUNE 9.00			:
	AUSTRIA v ITALY	PARIS SF	23 JUNE 4.00			:
	CAMEROON v CHILE	NANTES	23 JUNE 4.00			:
C	DENMARK v SAUDI ARABIA	LENS	12 JUNE 5.30			:
	FRANCE v S.AFRICA	MARSEILLE	12 JUNE 9.00			:
	DENMARK v S.AFRICA	TOULOUSE	18 JUNE 5.30			:
	FRANCE v SAUDI ARABIA	PARIS SF	18 JUNE 9.00			:
	DENMARK v FRANCE	LYON	24 JUNE 4.00			:
	SAUDI ARABIA v S.AFRICA	BORDEAUX	24 JUNE 4.00			:
D	BULGARIA v PARAGUAY	MONTPELLIER	12 JUNE 2.30			:
	NIGERIA v SPAIN	NANTES	13 JUNE 2.30			:
	BULGARIA v NIGERIA	PARIS PP	19 JUNE 5.30			:
	PARAGUAY v SPAIN	ST ÉTIENNE	19 JUNE 9.00			:
	BULGARIA v SPAIN	LENS	24 JUNE 9.00			:
	NIGERIA v PARAGUAY	TOULOUSE	24 JUNE 9.00			:
E	MEXICO v SOUTH KOREA	LYON	13 JUNE 5.30			:
	BELGIUM v HOLLAND	PARIS SF	13 JUNE 9.00			:
	BELGIUM v MEXICO	BORDEAUX	20 JUNE 5.30			:
	HOLLAND v SOUTH KOREA	MARSEILLE	20 JUNE 9.00			:
	HOLLAND v MEXICO	ST ÉTIENNE	25 JUNE 4.00			:
	BELGIUM v SOUTH KOREA	PARIS PP	25 JUNE 4.00			:
F	IRAN v YUGOSLAVIA	ST ÉTIENNE	14 JUNE 5.30			:
	GERMANY v USA	PARIS PP	15 JUNE 9.00			:
	GERMANY v YUGOSLAVIA	LENS	21 JUNE 2.30			:
	IRAN v USA	LYON	21 JUNE 9.00			:
	GERMANY v IRAN	MONTPELLIER	25 JUNE 9.00			:
	USA v YUGOSLAVIA	NANTES	25 JUNE 9.00			:
G	ENGLAND v TUNISIA	MARSEILLE	15 JUNE 2.30			:
	COLOMBIA v ROMANIA	LYON	15 JUNE 5.30			:
	COLOMBIA v TUNISIA	MONTPELLIER	22 JUNE 2.30			:
	ENGLAND v ROMANIA	TOULOUSE	22 JUNE 5.30			:
	ROMANIA v TUNISIA	PARIS SF	26 JUNE 9.00			:
	COLOMBIA v ENGLAND	LENS	26 JUNE 9.00			:
H	ARGENTINA v JAPAN	TOULOUSE	14 JUNE 2.30			:
	CROATIA v JAMAICA	LENS	14 JUNE 9.00			:
	CROATIA v JAPAN	NANTES	20 JUNE 2.30			:
	ARGENTINA v JAMAICA	PARIS PP	21 JUNE 5.30			:
	ARGENTINA v CROATIA	BORDEAUX	26 JUNE 4.00			:
	JAMAICA v JAPAN	LYON	26 JUNE 4.00			:

SECOND ROUND

1 — PARIS PP 27 JUNE 9.00
WINNER OF A
RUNNER-UP OF B
WINNER ___ SCORE ___

2 — MARSEILLE 27 JUNE 4.30
WINNER OF B
RUNNER-UP OF A
WINNER ___ SCORE ___

3 — LENS 28 JUNE 4.30
WINNER OF C
RUNNER-UP OF D
WINNER ___ SCORE ___

4 — PARIS SF 28 JUNE 9.00
WINNER OF D
RUNNER-UP OF C
WINNER ___ SCORE ___

5 — TOULOUSE 29 JUNE 9.00
WINNER OF E
RUNNER-UP OF F
WINNER ___ SCORE ___

6 — MONTPELLIER 29 JUNE 4.30
WINNER OF F
RUNNER-UP OF E
WINNER ___ SCORE ___

7 — BORDEAUX 30 JUNE 4.30
WINNER OF G
RUNNER-UP OF H
WINNER ___ SCORE ___

8 — ST ÉTIENNE 30 JUNE 9.00
WINNER OF H
RUNNER-UP OF G
WINNER ___ SCORE ___

QUARTER-FINALS

A — NANTES 3 JULY 9.00
WINNER OF 1
WINNER OF 4
WINNER ___ SCORE ___

B — PARIS SF 3 JULY 4.30
WINNER OF 2
WINNER OF 3
WINNER ___ SCORE ___

C — MARSEILLE 4 JULY 4.30
WINNER OF 5
WINNER OF 8
WINNER ___ SCORE ___

D — LYON 4 JULY 9.00
WINNER OF 6
WINNER OF 7
WINNER ___ SCORE ___

SEMI-FINALS

MARSEILLE 7 JULY 9.00
WINNER OF A
WINNER OF C
WINNER ___ SCORE ___

PARIS SF 8 JULY 9.00
WINNER OF B
WINNER OF D
WINNER ___ SCORE ___

THIRD PLACE FINAL
PARIS PP 11 JULY 9.00
___
WINNER ___ SCORE ___

WORLD CUP FINAL
PARIS SF 12 JULY 9.00
___

WORLD CHAMPIONS